AUDUBON'S BUTTERFLIES, MOTHS, AND OTHER STUDIES

By Alice Ford

Audubon's Animals
Audubon's Butterflies, Moths, and Other Studies
Pictorial Folk Art
Edward Hicks, Painter of the Peaceable Kingdom

AUDUBON'S

BUTTERFLIES, MOTHS,
AND OTHER STUDIES

compiled and edited by
ALICE FORD

THE STUDIO PUBLICATIONS, INC.
in association with
THOMAS Y. CROWELL COMPANY
New York and London

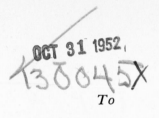

To

MRS. KIRBY CHAMBERS,

through whose generous cooperation the public is enabled
to share her exceptional Audubon sketchbook, heretofore
unknown and unpublished, and never exhibited before its
appearance in these pages.

CONTENTS

ACKNOWLEDGMENTS

IN 1942 Mrs. Kirby Chambers of New Castle, Kentucky, acquired Audubon's sketchbook from a descendant of the Basham family, to whom the painter had presented it in 1824. Thanks to her kindness, it is now possible for nature lovers, connoisseurs, and others to enjoy this fifteen-page pioneer art rarity. Editor and publisher join in expressing the utmost thanks to Mrs. Chambers for making the sketches available for publication.

The Charleston Museum, which forwarded Miss Maria Martin's two original sketchbooks of insects for study and reproduction, made a sterling contribution to the scope of this book. Mr. E. Milby Burton, Director, and Miss Emma B. Richardson of the museum deserve grateful mention.

The Pierpont Morgan Library, of New York, rendered valuable service. Mr. Frederick B. Adams, Jr., Director, gave generously of his time and excellent counsel. Mrs. Minnie Horowitz, authority on water-color technique and preservation, provided interesting and helpful information as to Audubon's painting methods as exemplified in the sketchbook. Mr. Mark D. Brewer, Photographer, photographed all the latter, as well as items illustrated from Maria Martin's sketchbook.

At the American Museum of Natural History, New York, Mr. John C. Pallister, of the Department of Entomology, identified the spiders and all insects except the butterflies. Mrs. Bessie Hecht, of the Department of Reptiles, also helped with identification. Miss Hazel Gay, Museum Librarian, and her staff assisted with research.

Mr. Stanley Clisby Arthur, Audubon biographer and scholar of note, helped signally by lending his extensive correspondence of the 1930's concerning the sketchbook's history. Mr. Arthur also turned over for reference a complete transcript, made some years ago, of Audubon's penciled annotations on the original paintings of *The Birds of America,* a number of which pertain to the insect and botanical accessories.

Dr. William E. Lingelbach, Librarian of the American Philosophical Society, Philadelphia, granted permission to quote from unpublished pages of an Audubon journal. Mrs. Ruth Duncan, Assistant, aided with research, as did Mr. Willman Spawn, Restorer.

The Houghton Library of Harvard University opened its exceptional collection of letters, manuscripts, and drawings by Audubon. I am particularly obliged to Mr. William A. Jackson, Librarian, Miss Caroline Jakeman, Assistant, and Mr. G. W. Cottrell, Jr., Editor.

To The Cooper Union Museum Library, of New York, goes grateful recognition for allowing the reproduction of eighteen aquatints from its Folio of *The Birds of America,* a handsome, beautifully preserved set once in the collection of Mr. Erskine Hewitt, grandson of Mr. Peter Cooper, founder of The Cooper Union. I should like to thank Miss Gerd Muehsam, Associate Librarian, Mr. Whitney N. Morgan, Assistant Museum Librarian, and Mr. Horace Hotchkiss, Museum Assistant, for their valuable aid. Mr. George N. Cowdery photographed the plates for the library.

At the Smithsonian Institution, Miss Elizabeth H. Gazin, Chief of Library Reference and Circulation, aided with research and also introduced me to Dr. Doris M. Cochran and Messrs. Austin H. Clark and John F. G. Clarke, zoologists, who identified certain reptiles and butterflies. In further consultation Mr. Clark and Mr. William D. Field identified all of the latter, as given.

Mr. Bryan Holme, of The Studio Publications, is entitled to a large measure of grateful appreciation for sharing my wish to bring the sketchbook before the public; and he is responsible for its completely faithful and truly beautiful reproduction and presentation.

Others deserving of thanks for various valued services include the following: Miss Harriet Chambers; Mr. Thomas B. Chambers; The Carnegie Library of Pittsburgh and Miss Rose Demorest, Librarian of the Pennsylvania Room; Mr. Howard Corning; Mrs. Frances H. J. Coffin; Mrs. Grange S. Coffin; The Cincinnati Public Library and Miss Ethel L. Hutchins, Reference Librarian; The Club of Odd Volumes, Boston; Mrs. Peter Edson; The Filson Club of Louisville, and Miss Ludie Kinkead, Curator; The James MacDonald Company, New York; The National Audubon Society and Mrs. Monica A. De La Salle, Librarian; The New York Public Library; The Old Print Shop, New York (from whose originals the color plates of the *Birds* details were reproduced); and The William Henry Smith Memorial Library of Indianapolis.

For their color research and expert craftsmanship, thanks are due to Powers Photo Engraving Company and to Messrs. Charles A. Powers and S. D. Faber for their special supervision. Thanks are also due to The Cornwall Press, Inc., for the printing of the text and to Civic Printing Co., Inc., for the printing of the illustrations.

Passages from Audubon were slightly edited in the interest both of readability and taste. Pleonastic sentences and endless paragraphs were converted to a series. Parenthetical effusions and period mannerisms were here and there deleted. More than a century of intensive alteration of the naturalist's published prose preceded this comparatively modest and restrained activity. Much of the original editing went on with the naturalist's personal approval and direction; but, even so, signs of his century's curious admixture of the unconsciously cruel and the errantly sentimental persisted. The paradox was a Romantic and Victorian characteristic, to be witnessed in the vast painted and literary output of that era. Squeamish though he was, William MacGillivray, scientific ghost writer who edited Audubon's "episodes" and *Ornithological Biography,* suffered much to be printed toward which today's reader might well exhibit slight tolerance. The professor took judicious liberties on the whole, however, adding only flourishes of his own to Audubon's already florid style. John Bachman, Maria Martin, and Audubon's two sons did well in editing the *Quadrupeds.* An editor's sense of responsibility to the original writer, if it be deep and lively, will also safeguard the interests of the reader. He who serves one, inevitably manages to serve the other.

ALICE FORD

I

AUDUBON'S BIRTH

Truth and Legend

JOHN JAMES AUDUBON himself sowed the seed of the Lost Dauphin legend. The idea that he may have been the little son of Marie Antoinette and Louis XVI who was spirited from Temple prison in Paris during the Revolution took root in the minds of the painter's descendants.

Most of his granddaughters believed that his papers proved him to be "The Dauphin." Only one, who died in 1947, the last of her generation, scoffed mildly at such an idea. Her sister, however, had earlier turned over to Stanley Clisby Arthur, one of Audubon's recent biographers, certain diary notes hinting at royal birth. This action was prompted by displeasure with a biography by Francis Hobart Herrick, *Audubon the Naturalist,* published in 1917, and reissued in 1938 with a lengthy introduction disputing the dauphin theory. With scholarly rectitude Herrick revealed the tale of Audubon's emergence, out of wedlock, in Santo Domingo on April 26, 1785, as the son of Captain John Audubon, French navy officer and planter, and one Mademoiselle Rabin, wealthy Creole of genteel background. Arthur, in 1937, presented the dramatic suppressed lines of the diary, while leaving the way open for any new revelations. But he inclined meanwhile to side with Herrick's sensational findings.

Like the woodsman that Audubon was, he took pains, it appears, to close the path to the full Santo Domingo story. Backtracking at fairly long intervals, he gave conflicting versions concerning his beginnings, lest his fame be dimmed by consequence of truth. He wished no stigma to touch his sons or the family name.

In his brief autobiography, "Myself," he declared he could only repeat what he had heard his father tell of his birth on a large Santo Domingo plantation, to a beautiful and rich lady of Spanish extraction whom the Captain had met and married in New Orleans. He declared that he had two brothers and that his mother had died young during a period of Negro insurrection on the island. Audubon and his half sister Rosa—child of a union that followed his own mother's death—departed with their father for France. Captain Audubon's lawful wedded wife, a widow whom he had married seven years before, kindly Ann Moynet, welcomed him and his charges in Nantes. The childless woman took the children to her heart, with legal adoption the natural outcome.

At another time, in the preface of his *Ornithological Biography*, Audubon vaguely designated "the New World" as his birthplace, but in the text he once referred to his "native Louisiana."

In a letter to his wife in 1827 he spoke of New Orleans as his "natal city." Yet on a different occasion, during the years he lived abroad while publishing his *Birds*, he wrote of an excursion to Versailles as though he were returning to old familiar haunts. He dropped hints of being the one "who should command all!" while humbly, perforce, roaming the streets of France as a "common man." Another time, in a suppressed passage in his journal, he alluded to his resemblance to his *"real"* father, which he noticed one morning while shaving. There are, on the other hand, additional instances where he remarked upon his likeness to Captain Audubon.

Apparently Audubon derived a sly enjoyment from obscuring the record, or at least this is suggested by certain of his more preposterous assurances to credulous persons met by the wayside. One such acquaintance recorded a statement in her diary to the effect that he was born on the lower Mississippi's banks in Louisiana—not only that, but in a cottage set in an orange grove! Another time, whiling away an evening on a Mississippi flatboat, he amused himself in the company of Vincent Nölte, the well-known European merchant. Nölte, who later published an account of the meeting, said Audubon was wearing a bandanna on his head, French sailor fashion, causing him to guess his nationality as Gallic. When Audubon replied, "Hi emm an Heenglishman," Nölte naturally remarked that an Englishman would hardly speak with such an accent. The explanation was given with much laughter: "Hi emm Heenglish becaz hi got a Heenglish wife!" Then with all seriousness Audubon added that he was a native of La Rochelle, France, but that he belonged to "every country."

One of his censored journals intimates cryptically that Captain Audubon had sworn the painter to secrecy in his youth, an oath from which he would gladly have been absolved, or so he said. Whatever the real secret of his birth, Lucy Audubon, his wife, was apprised of it. And whatever it may have been, it died with her, for she never confided it to her sons. Yet perhaps it is worth noting that every one of his conflicting statements, spoken and written over a period of many years, was made by him after his marriage, when his real identity began to matter.

In his journal of 1820, which coincides with the colorful period when Audubon made most of the studies reproduced in this book, the artist for once gave an account of his birth which more nearly tallies with documented facts than any other of his statements. On November 28 of that year he wrote:

"As it is a rainy morning, I cannot hunt, and will take this opportunity to relate such incidents relative to my life as I think my family may at some future period be glad to know.

"My father, John Audubon, was born at Sables D'Olorme in France, the son of a man who had a very large family, there being twenty males and one female. His father started him at a very early age as a cabin boy on board a whaling ship. Of course, by education, he was nothing; but he was naturally quick, industrious and soberly inclined. . . . He soon became able to command a fishing smack, to purchase it, and proceed on the road to Fortune. When of age, he commanded a small vessel belonging to him, trading to Santo Domingo. . . . He entered as an officer in the French Navy's service under Louis XVI, and was employed as agent at Santo Domingo to carry on trade. . . . He became wealthy.

"The American Revolution brought him to this country as commander of a frigate under the Count Rochambeau. He had the honor of being presented to the great Washington. And Major Croghan of Kentucky, who has told me often that he then looked much like me, was particularly well acquainted with him. My father was in several engagements in the American service and at the taking of Lord Cornwallis. Before his return to Europe he purchased a beautiful farm in Pennsylvania.

"The civil wars of France and Santo Domingo brought such heavy ravages of fortune on his head that it was with the utmost difficulty that his life was spared. He, along with thousands, now saw his wealth torn from him, and he had little more left than was necessary to live and educate two children left out of five. . . . The French navy prospered not, and he retired to a small but beautiful country seat three leagues from Nantes in sight of the Loire River, and there his life ended happy. . . . His generosity was often too great. As a father I never complained of him, and the many durable friends he had prove him to have been a good man.

"My mother, who, I have been told, was an extraordinarily beautiful woman, died shortly after my birth, and, my father having remarried in France, I was removed thereto when only two years old [actually four] and received by that best of women [Ann Moynet], and raised and cherished by her. My father gave me and my sister Rosa an education appropriate to his purse. . . . I perhaps would have stored up much [learning] if the continual wars in which France was engaged had not forced me away when only fourteen years old. I entered the Navy and was received as a Midshipman at Rochefort, much against my inclinations. The short peace of 1802 between England and France ended my military career. But the conscription determined my father on sending me to America to live on the farm, 'Mill Grove.'

"He sent me to the care of Miers Fisher, a rich and honest Quaker of Philadelphia, his agent for many years. A young man of seventeen, sent to America to make money, brought up in France in easy circumstances . . . I was ill fitted for it. I spent much money and one year of my life as happy as the young bird that, having left the parents' sight, carols merrily, while hawks are watching him for easy prey. I had a partner with whom I did not agree. . . . We parted forever. I should have mentioned that when I landed in New York I took the yellow fever and did not reach Philadelphia for three months.

"Shortly after my arrival on my farm, Lucy Bakewell came [from England] with her father's family to a farm called 'Fatland Ford,' divided from mine only by the Philadelphia Road. We soon became acquainted and I became attached to her. I went to France to obtain my father's consent to marry her, and returned with a business partner, Ferdinand Rozier of

Nantes. . . . I travelled through the Western country and made Louisville my choice for a residence. On my return, being of age, I married [Lucy Bakewell] in 1808 and removed to Kentucky. . . ."

Almost all of the dozen years preceding 1821 are a recital of his financial failures. Between his abiding confidence in the worthiness of his ambition to portray all the birds of North America and his continuous labors to perfect his style and method, there are the annals of his commercial failures in Kentucky; his desperate attempts to support his growing family; and—after utter defeat and disgrace from bankruptcy in Henderson—his penniless, despondent walk to Louisville, where he tried to subsist on sketching black chalk portraits. After Lucy and their boys, Victor and John, joined him, they were obliged to find shelter with friends. His discouragement deepened upon the death of an infant daughter, born shortly after Lucy's arrival. Not so very long before, they had buried another girl child named Lucy, at Spring Garden, plantation of General Samuel Hopkins near Henderson, Kentucky.

With the offer and acceptance of the job of "stuffing fishes" for the Western Museum in Cincinnati, Audubon's luck appeared to have taken an upward turn. But the handsome monthly wage of $125 was seldom paid him, and he was soon obliged to seek other work to supplement his precarious income as a taxidermist. His perseverance was not without its reward because, through the drawing school that he founded, he discovered the useful talents of a most unusual pupil. Thirteen-year-old Joseph Robert Mason, whose budding gifts as a botanical painter inspired Audubon's close supervision and special interest, was soon to figure importantly in his destiny. The two prowled the woods together with their sketchbooks, and young Mason's knowledge of flowers proved highly beneficial. When Audubon became convinced that the uncertainties of existence in Cincinnati were leading him nowhere, and that he might better travel south to complete his birds, the lad went along as his assistant. Under Audubon's exacting direction he sketched a goodly number of the floral habitats for the master's birds. This was during Audubon's most distinguished painting period, from which emerged not only many portraits for the *Birds of America,* together with their entomological details, but also the sketches of insects and small reptiles hitherto unpublished. Mason, too, painted insects, such as the wasp pursued by the yellow-throated vireo on page 65.

II

THE SKETCHBOOK

A Brief History

AUDUBON'S SKETCHBOOK may be regarded as the rare and beautiful collateral of his *Birds of America,* the monumental work which made him famous. According to the family record of the Bashams, the owners of the sketchbook for generations, and as the watermarks of the sketchbook and other facts testify, the artist began his sketches in 1821. Audubon was then thirty-six, still struggling, moving tenuously from one teaching engagement to another, steadfast only to his bird collecting and drawing.

Most of the butterflies and three of the reptiles were evidently acquired via the port of New Orleans, or from collectors such as Audubon's letters and journals of various periods frequently mention.

This little-known sketchbook of fifteen pages of insects and reptiles, drawn in water color in their natural size, matches in technical brilliance and virtuosity, artistically speaking, any of Audubon's birds of the same period, generally acknowledged to be his greatest. When the artist started out for Louisville in October, 1823, en route to Philadephia to try to win the support of naturalists in his vast undertaking vis-à-vis the birds, he shipped his portfolio ahead of him. The sketchbook went either with him or with that shipment.

In October, 1824, much indebted to Mrs. Charles Basham and her daughter Harriet for all their kindness during his indigent stay in Pittsburgh, Audubon was hard put to it to repay them. The cash for a farewell remembrance was not at hand. Then it was that he decided on the handsome presentation of the sketchbook as a gift to the Bashams.

The painter's account of his last call on the Bashams in Pittsburgh, to deliver the sketchbook and a farewell letter the day before his departure down the Ohio, was burned more than half a century ago. Apprehensive of the wisdom of sharing with posterity Audubon's "bitter" record of hardships endured in 1822-1824, the naturalist's granddaughter, Maria R. Audubon, threw the journals for these years in the fire. An innocuous passage or two is all that remains, these having been preserved through biographies by Buchanan and the painter's wife not long after his death. These passages, it must be regretfully added, were liberally altered to suit the editors' notions of propriety. In view of these events, it is all the more fortunate that Mrs. Basham's memoirs survive, for they help reconstruct the story of the sketchbook.

Mrs. Basham, a native of County Cavan, Ireland, and wife of an Englishman who settled in America, abstracted portions of her earlier journals to form her memoirs in the year 1871. By then she was living in Louisville, her final home, having moved about from city to city in the East following her departure from Pittsburgh around 1826. Little is known concerning her husband's profession or personal history, but her own activities, including conversations with Audubon, Burr, and others, she herself accounted for fully. Even had she failed to do so, traces of her life remain in Pittsburgh archives.

A notice of the opening of general classes "attended by Mrs. Basham" at "The School" in Pittsburgh, located at "the corner of Fourth and Wood Streets," appeared in the *Gazette* on August 29, 1823. It reappeared the following year about a month before Audubon walked into the city from Meadville, accompanied by a vagabond artist met during his return journey from Ontario. "The School" was directed by a board of two clergymen and two other Pittsburgh citizens. In 1824, just before Audubon arrived, the school had appointed an art teacher to its staff, R. J. Lambdin, but this did not deter Mrs. Basham from engaging the naturalist to give her daughter private lessons, once she had met him and seen for herself the loveliness of the flowers painted as habitats for his birds. Her daughter, Miss Harriet, then about sixteen, excelled at botanical painting, a talent which her mother and "Mr. Audubon" encouraged.

His money all but gone and his soles worn thin from days of walking toward the river, only to learn in Pittsburgh that he must wait for the rising of the Ohio's waters before heading for New Orleans and his waiting Lucy, Audubon welcomed the appointment. During his six weeks in the city, his time was taken up with teaching and portrait sketching, but no friends were as loyal and understanding as the Bashams. They constantly invited him to their home for meals and on social occasions to meet their many friends.

The daughter of Harriet Basham, Mrs. Bowen of Louisville, willed the sketchbook to her daughter Bertha Bowen, also of that city. Until a few years ago, when it was acquired by a friend, Mrs. Kirby Chambers of New Castle and Louisville, it remained with Miss Bowen. The writer became aware of its possible existence by means of a "note" in a highly successful story of 1936—Constance Rourke's *Audubon*, which mentioned the "butterflies, dragonflies and lizards made by Audubon during the early part of his stay in Feliciana." The word *early* was employed in the sense that the painter returned to that parish in 1825 before departing for extended residence in Britain.

In October, 1931, when Miss Bowen finally decided to part with her precious heirloom, she wrote to Mr. Stanley Clisby Arthur. Her letter to the biographer referred not only to the sketches but to her great-grandmother's journals and memoirs. "I am the fourth generation to own these treasures," she said, "and as there is no one to succeed me I should like to dispose of them. I have also a letter written by Audubon to Mrs. Basham, which partly fell to pieces when I opened it three years ago, but his signature is intact, and also the date, October 23, 1824. . . . Pieces had been lost by some of the Audubon family who borrowed it to examine and read." Upon transfer of the album to the present owner, the precious autograph and date went with it. The rest of "the much decayed letter" remained with Miss Bowen.

Mrs. Basham's decision to draft her memoirs from her journal came about when friends had convinced her that hers had been no ordinary life. So, in 1871, she was persuaded to copy from her journals her first record of the painter's six weeks' stay in Pittsburgh. She mentioned how he had allowed her to make a copy of his draft of an episode later published, "Meadville," which described his experiences in that Pennsylvania village a few days before he set out on his ninety-mile walk to Pittsburgh. Mrs. Basham quaintly alluded to this story, which is almost identical with the final printed version, as "a narrative of Mr. Audubon in quest of birds, minus cash, shewing his simplicity."

"In Pittsburgh he charmed all who saw him," Mrs. Basham reminisced. "Mr. Audubon has made himself so well known in the world that any mention of him is superfluous. As he permitted me to read his narrative [forty-seven] years since, I take a kind of doting gratification copying it at this late date. He had not then a copy of the work [the *Birds of America*] that he was then struggling to prepare, which would have the patronage of kings and princes, nor little thought of his future greatness. . . . [I was] induced, perhaps foolishly, to copy what I had written forty-seven years since, from the feeling that few have risen to the pinnacle of fame as Mr. Audubon from the penniless traveller in Meadville, to be the associate of kings and emperors. As proof—not long since, his snuff box from Emperor Alexander was sent here to be raffled.[1]

"On October 24, Mr. Audubon called to say adieu, and brought . . . his drawings to Harriet, having given her lessons in drawing.

"He had returned to Pittsburgh on account of low water, and now placed himself, drawings and friend in a skiff for New Orleans. This friend, Dr. La Motte, fled from France in Charles the Tenth's reign and had a letter from Lafayette to Mr. [James] Ross, one of our great lawyers. On Lafayette's visiting Pittsburgh [in 1825] he spoke of Dr. La Motte . . . who was going to Mexico to cure a disease called 'guitre' [goiter]. Alas, he, on his arrival there, died of yellow fever. . . .

"Mr. Audubon wished to see Mrs. Adams, then upwards of 100, and living in the third house built in Pittsburgh. For the past several years [she had] received the premium for fine stockings, having spun and knit them, but she could not be persuaded to dispose of a pair to Mr. Audubon. . . .

"In [1844],[2] when on a visit to New York, I heard he had a fine place on the North River, and found him pleasantly situated near Manhattan. He called on me in return but I was out. He took us to see his workshop where

[1] During a visit to London, the Emperor of Russia presented Audubon with a gold snuff box studded with diamonds.

[2] Audubon died in 1851. His buffalo calf drawing was made at Fort Union in 1843 on his Upper Missouri expedition. Therefore, Mrs. Basham's visit was about 1844, though she recalled it, when she herself was far advanced in years, as 1852.

stood a buffalo calf [drawing]. Having finished the birds, he was interested in beasts.

"He was keenly sensitive. When he was in Pittsburgh, one of the great men, Babcock, called to have a crayon sketch [made of himself], saying 'Now don't ask much for it, Mr. Audubon.' Audubon replied, 'At present, sir, I am engaged with my birds. I have to decline the honor—money is no inducement—none Sir!' He was then drawing a branch with live wild pigeons caught on Grant's Hill—as seen at Cooper's Institute [in New York] as well as in Washington in his immense books."

From the point of view of his bird collection, Audubon's Pittsburgh visit was none too productive. But, had he accomplished nothing else, his "Passenger Pigeon," referred to in Mrs. Basham's memoirs, a beautiful painting of a tenderly loving pair of that now long extinct species, might well have secured his reputation. Mrs. Basham's visit with Audubon at his country home, Minnies Land, that day in the mid-1840's, coincided with the time when he was hard at work on his second and last monumental venture, *The Viviparous Quadrupeds of North America*.

The Beauty of the Sketches

To invest the exquisite figures of the sketchbook with a miniaturelike quality of aliveness, Audubon cunningly devised different technical means to achieve this end. Much detail can be seen to advantage with a microscope, suggesting that he may have used a magnifying glass to aid him in much of the work. No infinitesimal part of insect, or intricate surface pattern of reptile, escaped his attention, even where he chose to conventionalize the designs on the surface of some of the creatures in a free and creatively symbolic manner. He did not pin or pose them all in the customary way.

In the first and only published discussion of Audubon's insects, Edwin Way Teale, apparently unaware of the existence of the sketchbook, made some interesting observations about the insect details in the *Birds of America*. In an article in the *Audubon Magazine* he wrote in 1947: "Of the 435 pictures in Audubon's great work, more than half a hundred contain insects as well as birds. They cover a wide range. . . . In a few cases, the insects are drawn with such exactness and colored with such care that frequently they can be identified not only as to family but as to species as well." The same is true of the figures in the sketchbook, some of which are precise enough for the most exacting scientific scrutiny. Others tend toward the impressionistic or symbolic, because of the scientifically unsophisticated era of their creation, and because, too (as was emphasized in *Audubon's Animals*), the creator is to be regarded as a naturalist in a limited sense only, as genuine ornithologist and zoologist never, but as an *artist* of unchallenged genius, first and last. The discovery of the sketchbook forcibly supports

BUTTERFLY, *Pararge aegeria* (Linné).

PAINTED LADY BUTTERFLY, *Vanessa cardui* (Linné).

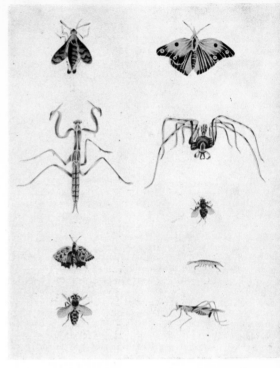

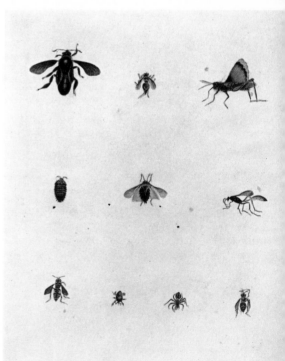

Five pages from Audubon's sketchbook. Facsimile-size reproductions of details appear in color on page 17, and subsequently both in color and black and white. All the illustrations from the remaining ten pages of the sketchbook are also reproduced in facsimile size on pages 20 through 24, and on pages 33 through 40. The reptiles contained in the sketchbook appear on pages 97 through 100. The sketches were done between the years 1821 and 1823, when Audubon spent most of his time in the region of New Orleans, West

Feliciana, and Natchez. Identification of the species reveals that the artist must have been equally fascinated by certain foreign specimens brought to this country via New Orleans or other ports, as well as by those that are native to our own shores. Audubon presented this collection to Mrs. Charles Basham and her daughter Harriet in Pittsburgh on October 24, 1824. The sketchbook was acquired in 1942 by Mrs. Kirby Chambers from the Bashams' direct descendant, Miss Bertha Bowen. It is through the present owner's gracious permission that the work is reproduced for the first time in this book.

Above: BUTTERFLY, *Hamearis lucina* (Linné). FLY.
Left: MOTH. *Below*: *left*,
B E E T L E. *Center*,
GROUND CRICKET.
Right, PLUME MOTH (?).
Opposite page, top:
MOTH, *Macroglossum stellatarum* (Linné). BUT-
TERFLY, *Colias croceus*
(Fourcroy). *Bottom*: BUT-
TERFLY, *Minois semele*
(Linné).

20

FLY.

Opposite page:
Left panel, top to bottom: CABBAGE BUTTER-
FLY. CENTIPEDE. SPIDER. GROUND BEETLE.
GROUND BEETLE. *Center panel*: GECKO, *Hemi-
dactylus*. GROUND BEETLE. *Right panel*: PRAY-
ING MANTIS (with details sketched above).
PRAYING MANTIS (with details sketched below).
GROUND BEETLE.

Left: SPHINX MOTH LARVA (fragment of ventral view). *Right*: DRAGONFLY

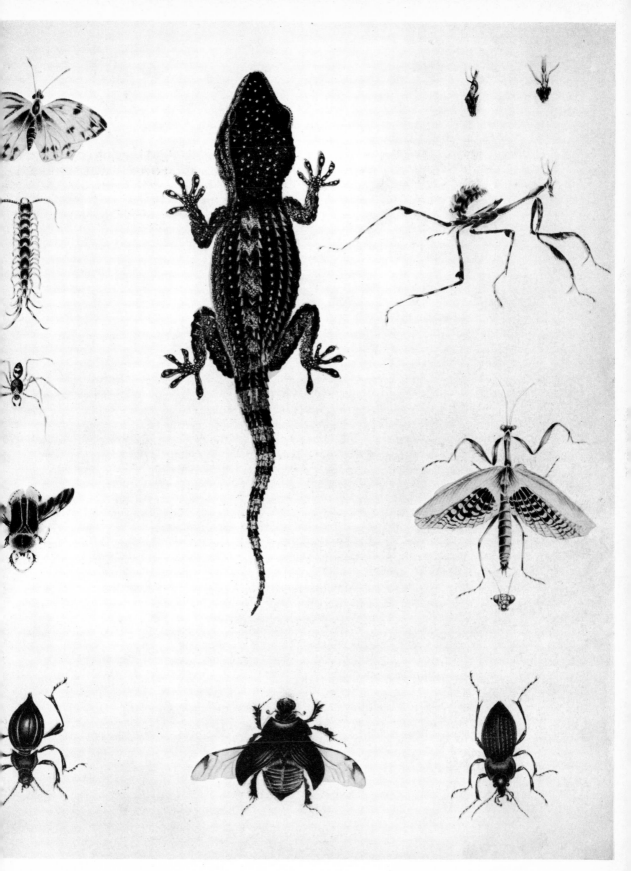

BUTTERFLY
Pieris Brassicae (Linné).

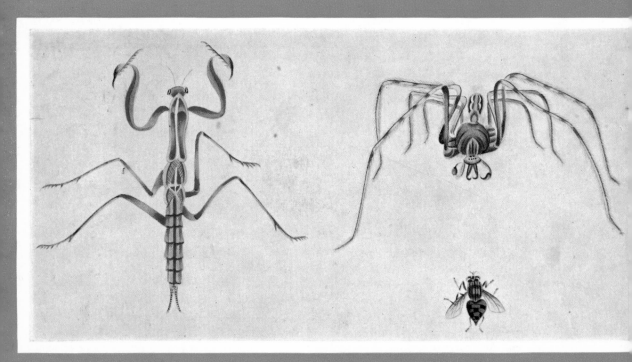

PRAYING MANTIS.   SPIDER.   FLY.

this contention, which scientists, often critical of his license, would do well to take to heart. Artists, from the beginning of time and to this very day, freely employ their creative prerogatives. No doubt they will continue to do so forever. Their work should therefore be appraised within its framework. Still, in defense of Audubon as a naturalist it may be noted that provocative differences of opinion were expressed, in some instances, by scientists who examined the creatures in the sketchbook.

In the lower Mississippi country late in 1820 Audubon's art reached full maturity. His earlier bird drawings had often been somewhat crude, with wing and head usually well enough finished but with tail perhaps only sketched in and left in a preliminary state, as if he had pressed on impatiently to his next subject, meaning to return. Just as there is no such restlessness evident in the bird renderings made in West Feliciana and the Natchez region, there is none—not a trace—in this sketchbook of the same period.

The watermarks on the imported English drawing papers he used indicate that the sketches were completed over a fairly extensive interval. "Basted Mill 1818," the mark discernible on four of the pages (some of them unpainted) was a paper apparently saved from an earlier supply. "Cansell 1820" is another of the watermarks. "J. Whatman 1822," the name of a house still famous for its fine papers and which Audubon favored throughout his career, is the third. All pages were loosely sewed in, as if added at different stages. These years, it must be remembered, were among Audubon's hardest; sometimes too poor to buy himself a journal for his daily records, he could only afford the most limited purchase of supplies. The marbled paper covers of the album of sketches are caught together at the opening with a faded and fraying ribbon.

One of the last pages bears an addition of recent years, the autograph of Harriet Audubon, granddaughter of the naturalist. During the time the sketchbook was in Miss Bowen's hands, Miss Audubon, also an artist, gave the Basham descendant painting lessons at the Belle Peers school in Louisville, and about twenty-five years ago was asked, for reasons of sentiment, to inscribe her name in the book.

When Audubon began work on the sketchbook he had already been seeking mastery of water-color technique as well as the use of pastel crayon for more than a quarter of a century. He added touches of black chalk and burnt cork, as required, having had experience with the latter while doing human portraits some time before in Kentucky. With the portraits, a stern kind of discipline, he relied consistently on what he remembered of his short tuition in Paris in boyhood under the celebrated Jacques Louis David, whose training stood him in good stead.

The insects and reptiles are all aqueous drawings, or washes, first marked out in pencil. To obtain his jewel-like effects the artist freely combined ink, water color, opaque white, and gold. He worked alternately with a pen and a fine brush, using both to apply ink and color over the penciled outlines. Crayon, being too coarse a medium for these luminous, tiny creatures, played no part in the creation—an interesting point in view of Audubon's long and extensive use of it, both before and after he worked on the sketch-book. His models forced him to experiment, and he did so with uncanny success.

One senses his fever to re-create, not simply to imitate or copy. Fidelity, according to his sometimes personal and fanciful concept, was his goal in transferring his impressions to paper, just as it was in his bird and mammal drawings. Butterfly, moth, beetle, and lizard are lifelike and vivid. Every one of the linear refinements of the centipede, woodland cockroach, and large grasshopper is reported with receptivity and magical assurance. The nearly invisible hairs of the bee's yellow abdomen create an illusion of actual softness. The roseate stippling on the back of the graceful and harm-less snake lends aliveness to its pale green translucence. The small, many-lensed insect eyes, some of which see by night—see above and behind, and sidewise and forward—seem to gaze upward as if alive, almost as if the insects were about to move their wings and dart off the paper.

In the latter pages of the sketchbook, the Bufo toad, leathery and wet looking, a gold ring in its brilliant eye, seems nearly to palpitate. The little reptiles are like jewels that were once fashioned by the genius of Chinese craftsmen, as priceless facsimiles of creatures ordered by whim of mandarin and war lord. The wings of the flies, filaments of filigreelike refinement, were drawn with a needlelike pen or with a few hairs at the side of the finest of brushes, which, often, effect remarkable transparency. The spiders, some of them quite conventionalized, are like exquisite enameled brooches. The iridescence of the yellow-winged beetle was achieved by means of blue, shading off to green and red with gradations to red and violet, as with the painting of the feathered neck of the hummingbird. Another beetle was painted with mixed greens, browns, and black, with added touches of gold. Astonishingly real are the dragonfly's wings, done with black ink or paint, and with transparent, very aqueous blue water color, full use having been made of light intermingled with subtle coloring. Appraised as art, these drawings rank as diminutive masterpieces, unique in American illustration not only of their time but judged by any fair temporal standards.

The Period of the Sketchbook

Audubon's journal, begun on October 12, 1820, the date he left Cincin-nati, affords vivid glimpses of his fortunes and adventures, not only on the Ohio and Mississippi but in West Feliciana, New Orleans, and Natchez. His first entry reflects his apprehension and excitement as he set out on the long arduous journey, which was to result not only in the finest bird por-traits of his entire career but in the quintessential water-color drawings of the sketchbook as well.

"I left Cincinnati this afternoon at half past 4 o'clock, on board Mr.

Jacob Aumack's flat-boat—bound for New Orleans. The feeling of a husband and a father were my lot when I kissed my beloved wife and children with an expectation of being absent for seven months. I took with me Joseph Mason . . . and if God will grant us a safe return to our families, our wishes will be congenial to our present feelings, leaving home with a determined mind to fulfill our object. Without any money, my talents are to be my support and my enthusiasm my guide in my difficulties."

Audubon was not exaggerating when he said that he was entirely without funds. He had none whatever when he said good-by to Lucy, who planned to continue teaching in Cincinnati for the provision of both herself and their sons. Her classes had actually already contributed more than any of her husband's recent attempts to support the family. Lucy, the real breadwinner, early recognized the futility of trying to keep her visionary husband to a narrow course. With complete faith in his ultimate success, she encouraged, aided, and abetted all his aspirations.

Lightly though Audubon traveled, he found room for Linnaeus's book on natural history, which helps to account for the impressive scientific vocabulary used in his journal. He also carried with him as many of the late Alexander Wilson's volumes on American birds as were then obtainable, later writing at various times of his attempts to find the others in the bookshops of Natchez and New Orleans. Evidence of the wide scientific reading he did in his lifetime is to be found in his *Ornithological Biography,* in the text of the *Birds of America* which amends the former, and in his *Viviparous Quadrupeds of North America.*

Captain Samuel Cummings, a civil engineer, was aboard the flatboat with Audubon and Mason as far as Natchez. He was surveying the Mississippi for a book he later published—a popular standard guide till past midcentury. The friendship of Audubon and Cummings lasted throughout their lives, long after the painter's break with Mason. As they sailed along down the Ohio, they were a trio of rustics on the landscape, all three habitually without money. Audubon, whose hair fell in ringlets to his shoulders, promised himself to shave every Sunday. His rude leather clothing was replaced by nankeen when they reached the South. In the woods he always wore a hunter's knife at his side and carried a double-barreled rifle. On his back was a battered tin box of his drawings and colors, wrapped with his flute and fiddle in a blanket which he used at night for sleeping. Breck's *Recollections* reported that the painter had "the countenance of a bird . . . a projecting forehead, a sunken black eye, a parrot nose, and a long protruding chin, combined with an expression bold and eagle-like." Others marveled at his handsome though eaglelike appearance. Full maturity increased the strange resemblance to the bird, and once he even dreamed that he was one.

Much has been said, hinted, and decried concerning the family censorship of Audubon's journals. Especially to be deplored was Maria Audubon's rash burning of the 1822-1824 records. Fortunately certain passages survive from other sources besides the early biographies by Buchanan and Lucy Audubon. The American Philosophical Society of Philadelphia possesses the manuscript not only of "The Fair Incognito," an episode of romantic adventure with a New Orleans lady whom Audubon painted, but also some pages of the journal which Maria marked "Odd leaves of grandfather's journal, 1822— Not used and not for general reading as we decided." The pages, which are related to the period of the sketchbook, contain nothing in the least damaging. There is a little criticism of the New Orleans theater, reference to some "moon shining" in the local "coffee house" and a short entry about an hour or two spent watching the "roulette table" without taking part in the proceedings. Mention is made of a diet of maggoty cheese and cheap "salt mackerel." We find the dearth of portrait sitters deplored, this, like teaching, having been one means of earning a few dollars. Anxiety about Lucy and the boys, and annoyance with an "in-law" who might have offered to pay Audubon's passage to England, but did not, are also expressed. Tender and personal sentiments of the husband and lover who sometimes took umbrage were deemed censorable, as well as another allusion to "the Fair Incognito," about whom the artist had already told his wife in detail, forwarding her a copy of the episode itself with the warning not to show it to others, at least "for the present."

On the journey south, the forested banks of the Ohio and Mississippi, and oftentimes the skies above and the river swells below, were all astir with winged inspiration for Audubon's pencil. Partridge, woodcock, owl, thrush, buzzard, lark, robin, duck, fish hawk, godwit, wild turkey, dove, cormorant, goose, crane, heron, pecker, jay, grackle, crow, merganser, and kite flutter and dart through the pages of his journal.

When he, Mason, and Cummings were not slowly drifting downstream on Aumack's flatboat, with its captain, two passengers and rough crew of four, they were ashore in search of game. They would pause at squatters' huts and camps on the riverland borders and at far-scattered plantations to exchange news and stories. On board again, Audubon would spend entire days feverishly drawing birds, only occasionally taking the time to sketch the bluffs and scenery for diversion. Between them, though one wonders how they managed, he and Joseph purchased a skiff from a passing flatboat. They often floated ahead of Aumack's craft in the skiff, lying motionless in the bow when game was sighted. They used the light craft for excursions to shore, and up and down stream.

Leaving the Ohio behind and entering the Mississippi, Audubon wrote feelingly in mid-November:

"The 10th of May, 1819, I passed this place in an open skiff bound to New Orleans with two of my slaves. Now I enter it *poor*, in fact *Destitute* of all things, and relying only on that providential Hope, the comforter of this wearied mind. . . . The meeting of the two streams reminds me a little of the youth who comes in the world, spotless, and is gradually drawn into thousands of difficulties that make him wish to keep to himself, but at last he is mixed and lost in the Vortex. . . .

"I saw here two Indians in a canoe. They spoke some French, had bear traps, a few venison hams and a gun and looked so independent, free and unconcerned with the world that I gazed on them, admired their spirits, and wished for their condition. Here the traveller enters a new world; the current, about four miles per hour, puts the steersman on the alert and awakes him to troubles and difficulties unknown on the Ohio. The passenger feels a different atmosphere, a very different prospect. The curling stream and its hue are the first objects noticed. The caving in of the banks and the thick growth of young cottonwood is the next. The water's density reduced the thermometer from 62 to 20 degrees. We landed very early. Captain Cummings and I walked through the woods, and remarked the great difference of temperature so suddenly felt. I bid farewell to the Ohio at 2 o'clock P.M., and felt a fear gathering involuntarily. Every moment draws me away from all that is dear to me, my beloved wife and children."

He noted the appearance of "quantities of butterflies and other insects." His piercing "Indian eye" caught sight of an eagle's nest which he had seen a year and a half before in passing. He pointed out that migrating geese travel with the youngest or smallest in the center of their lines, the large gander leading the van and the oldest goose "driving the rear." Weather changes he also recorded with regularity. In the long evenings, feeling homesick as increasing distance separated him from Lucy, he would take out his portrait drawing to study her features, sometimes imagining that they had begun to assume an expression of sorrow or worry.

Entering the mouth of the White River, he went part way by boat, then on foot, to the "Post of Arkansas," an old fort once ruled by the Spanish dons, but by now an old, nearly deserted trading village. The tales he heard there from the Indians and trappers about the game and hunting at the Arkansas River's headwater country hundreds of miles northward filled Audubon with longing to reach it. He was already aspiring to make his bird drawings the most complete in existence, setting forth this aim in his journal by copying into it a letter he wrote to Governor Miller of the Arkansas territory:

"My ardent wish to complete a collection of drawings of the *Birds* of our country from *Nature,* all of natural size, begun about 15 years since . . . makes me wish to travel as far at least as the Osage nations on the Arkansas, as also along the whole of our frontiers." He was hinting to Miller for the chance to join any expedition that the official might be planning, but this tenacious dream was never to be realized. Rejoining Aumack and the others on the flatboat, he drifted on down to Natchez, arriving there two days after Christmas. His relative by marriage, Nicholas Berthoud, chanced to be there and offered him and Joseph a ride to New Orleans in his keelboat. Captain Cummings remained with Aumack.

Just as he was about to board Berthoud's craft, a nightmarish loss made Audubon "nearly sick." His portfolio containing fifteen bird drawings and Lucy's picture was carelessly put down on the river banks by a servant and left behind. For three anguished months the painter tried desperately by letter and message to trace the portfolio in New Orleans or to one of the many river boats that might have carried it away. He had abandoned hope when, in March, word arrived of its recovery, with only one drawing missing!

By New Year's he and Joseph were floating with Berthoud past fine Mississippi sugar and cotton plantations, rose gardens, and cypress groves. Through hanging Spanish moss darted grosbeaks, doves, sparrows, cuckoos, cardinals, bluebirds, goldfinches, wrens, catbirds, pewees, whippoorwills, nighthawks, and many of their brethren. Besides hosts of birds, Audubon took notice of many other kinds of creatures: "Some toads were hopping about this evening, and on turning a dead tree over we found several lizards who moved with great vigor." Again: ". . . In the swamps the crabs, young frogs, water snakes, &c. shew out in great numbers."

In New Orleans where the party landed on January 7, 1821, Audubon began at once to look for work. Lacking cash, he could do little to smooth his rough appearance. His worn breeches had been conspicuously mended by a squatter woman back on the Mississippi shores when the weather had turned bitter, at which time he had also lamented the lack of an outer jacket.

His easygoing ways acquired on the flatboat did little to further his aims in that city. Old acquaintances, embarrassed by his unkempt appearance, were often apt to pass him by. Yet his need was too pressing to allow that to daunt him. Despite his almost humble overtures, the portrait painter, John Jarvis, snubbed his offer to paint backgrounds for his canvases. Another well-established painter, John Vanderlyn, received Audubon more cordially but offered no practical assistance. Then, as fortune would have it, a wealthy planter named Mr. Pamar hired him as drawing teacher for members of his family, enabling him and Joseph to pursue their precious excursions to the woods for birds between times. Sudden prosperity followed from a steady flow of portrait commissions, effecting a happy change in his appearance and enabling him to go forth to his numerous appointments in a new, "dandified" suit of yellow nankeen. He sent a draft of $270 to Lucy and had a full set of crockery shipped to her. Throughout the painter's married life any upturn in his luck would always mean gifts for his family—such as a flute for Victor, a brooch, pianoforte, or necklace for Lucy. With exuberance he parted quickly with his gains.

One New Orleans citizen who hired his services was Madame André, who was the subject of "The Fair Incognito," already mentioned. The beautiful young widow paid him well for his two weeks of work on a drawing of her undraped person. At the end of the engagement she presented him with the finest double-barreled gun to be bought in the city, one which he personally selected. On it she had these words engraved in French: "Refuse not the gift of a grateful friend, and may it equal you yourself in goodness!" Under the ramrod could faintly be seen: "Property of LaForest Audubon, February 21, 1821." "LaForest" was also Lucy's favorite name for her husband, one which remains a cryptic part of his background.

Another appointment came through a physician, Louis Heerman, who, for his bored and restless wife, chose Audubon as drawing master, a move they were all to regret, as the painter's journal stresses. Repeated attempts to collect his fee for lessons to this fickle and flirtatious lady proved unavailing and resulted in a sharp, humiliating exchange with the doctor.

His adventures in New Orleans were many and varied. His episode "The Original Painter" tells of a chance meeting "on the *Levee*" one morning with a bizarrely attired artist. Not the least striking detail of his appearance was a "pink waistcoat, from the bosom of which, amidst a large bunch of the splendid flowers of the magnolia, protruded part of a young alligator." In one hand the gentleman held a cage full of finches, and in the other "he sported a silk umbrella on which were painted the words '*Stolen from I*' in large white characters." Audubon, naturally intrigued, ventured to speak to the stranger: "Sir, I am a student of nature, and admire her works, from the noblest figure of man to the crawling reptile which you have in your bosom." "Ah!" the artist replied, "a naturalist, I presume!" He offered to show his collection of "some more curious birds from different parts of the world," if Audubon would accompany him to his lodgings. After showing off his cages of birds, the painter announced that he would demonstrate "the *ne plus ultra* of shooting"; he then proceeded to shoot out the flame of a candle at "some yards," frightening the caged denizens of his studio.

"When light was restored," Audubon's episode runs, "I observed the uneasiness of the poor little alligator, as it strove to effect its escape from the artist's waistcoat. I mentioned this to him. 'True, true,' he replied, 'I had quite forgot the reptile; he shall have a dram'; and unbuttoning his vest, he unclasped a small chain, and placed the alligator in the basin of water on the table."

This story, interesting in itself, serves also as a reminder of the early colorful days of the port of New Orleans. Vessels plied between its bustling wharves and the West Indies and points south, bringing such exotic birds as the "Original Painter" collected. The snake and teeid, from the West Indies or South America, apparently came to be drawn at about this time, taking their places beside other specimens painted in and around Feliciana, New Orleans, and Natchez. The whiptail lizard must also have come in from the Far West with cargo, for countless sailing ships then plied between the teeming levees and the ports of Europe, South America, and the West Coast. The half dozen butterflies identified as European by Mr. Austin H. Clark may have entered the scene in the same fashion. Indeed, some of the other insects, particularly those of nearly universal incidence, could have been drawn by Audubon from specimens given him by one or more of the naturalists, both professional and amateur, whom he frequently met from the time of his arrival in America. Exchanges of knowledge and specimens from private collections were a nineteenth-century commonplace. Despite the Basham family's attestations about Feliciana as the sketchbook's provenance, it seems not implausible that some of the drawings may have dated back to Audubon's Western Museum days in Cincinnati, which, after all, immediately preceded his trip down the Ohio and Mississippi. Dr. Daniel Drake, the physician who headed the museum and who hired Audubon—the painter made a fine chalk likeness of him—collected *flora*, lectured on botany, and may possibly be linked to insects in the sketchbook adjudged European.

Audubon's acquaintance with Miss Elizabeth Pirrie, aged fifteen, proved of more serious consequence to his career than previous ones in the Louisiana capital. So successful were her first lessons that her delighted parents proposed that Audubon arrange to spend several months on their plantation, Oakley, so that she might benefit from intensive instruction. The painter would have preferred to go to Florida for birds, but for immediate practical reasons he decided to accept the Pirries' offer. He and Joseph Mason, who of course accompanied him, spent all their leisure hours tramping through the woodlands and swamps of the wonderful Bayou Sarah region of West Feliciana parish, 170 miles above New Orleans by river and 80 miles northwest, as the crow flies.

Audubon's artistry, stimulated by all the surrounding beauty and wild life, now entered a new and unsurpassed era, greatly productive and technically superb, not only as to birds but insects and reptiles. Turn to the pages of the sketchbook, as well as to certain details of the *Birds* finished in Feliciana—the exquisite "Blue Birds," for example, shown with a tiny caterpillar, on page 57, and also the "Ruby-throated Hummingbird" of mothlike proportions on page 61.

"The aspect of the country," Audubon wrote in his journal, "distracted my mind from those objects that are the occupation of my life. The rich magnolia covered with its odoriferous blossoms, the holly, the beech, the tall yellow poplar, the hilly ground, even the red clay I looked at with amazement. Such an entire change in so short a time appears often supernatural. Surrounded once more by thousands of warblers and thrushes, I enjoyed nature." Constantly he remarked upon insects in relation to the birds—the *"pinching* bug" with "two equal pairs of pincers," which was much to the chuck-will's-widow's taste; the beetles which the mockingbird first mesmerized by its melody then took as captive; the "ground crickets" and "scarabee" beetles which the wood ibis hunted.

His comfortable months on the Pirrie plantation permitted much freedom for his bird forays and sketching. Rarely does his journal report any serious interruption. However, one distracting event, reported with a certain wry humor, was occasioned by the death of a neighbor. Wakened out of his sleep, he hurried through the darkness to the bedside of the deceased, where he performed the somber task of sketching a posthumous portrait for the widow.

Audubon's nocturnal and daytime visits to the lovely lake five miles away are colorfully summed up in his account of the feeding habits of the wood ibis, a little gem of nature writing to be found later in the chapter, "Of Insects." No spider, insect, or other tiny creature escaped his eye. Not only did they provide new and endless fascination for him as he added one after another to his sketchbook, but they became an important part of many of his realistic bird compositions.

Late in August, Audubon and his pupil drew a rattlesnake, and his journal gives a full and most painstaking anatomical description of it. Some weeks later, when Elizabeth's health became too frail for the exertion of regular lessons, Audubon quarreled with her parents over their decision to

DRAGONFLY.

CARPENTER or BUMBLE BEE.   FLY.   GRASSHOPPER.

33

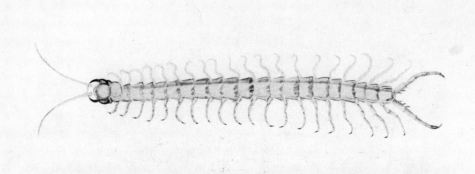

CENTIPEDE.

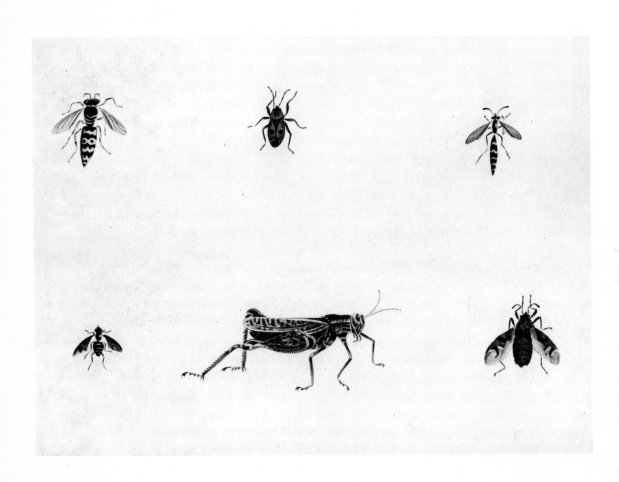

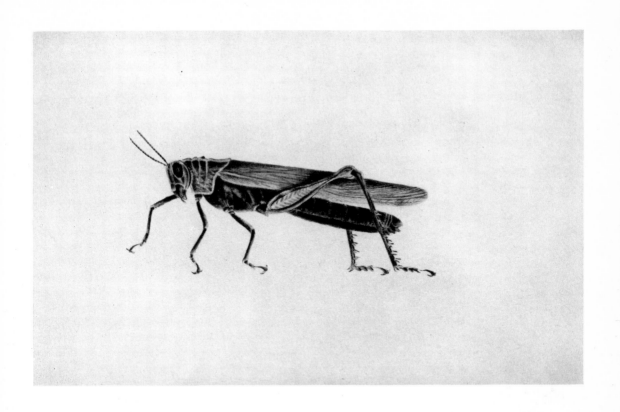

GRASSHOPPER, *Schistocerca americana.*

FLY.

Opposite page:
Top row, left to right: WASP (?). TRUE BUG. WASP.
Bottom row, left to right: TRUE BUG. GRASSHOPPER, *Melanoplus.* FLY.

35

Above, top row: FLY. BEE. *Second row*: BEE. FLY.
Opposite page:
Top row, left to right: WASP. COMMON FLY. FLY (wasp family). TAWNY
EMPEROR BUTTERFLY, *Asterocampa clyton* (Boisduval and Le Conte) or Euro-
pean species of *Argynnis*. *Second row*: GRASSHOPPER. CAMEL CRICKET.
TRUE BUG (Assassin). *Third row*: BEETLE. STINKBUG. STINKBUG. WASP.
BUMBLEBEE. *Fourth row*: MIDGE. WOOD COCKROACH. BUTTERFLY,
Pararge megaera (Linné).

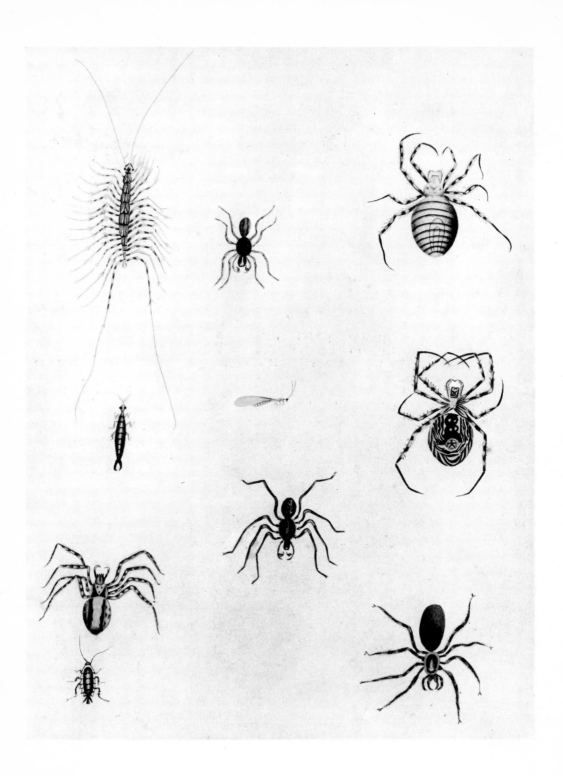

SOW BUG.   STINKBUG.   WASP.

Opposite page:

Left panel, top to bottom: HOUSE CENTIPEDE, *Scutigera forceps*. GROUND BEETLE, immature specimen. HUNTING SPIDER. WOOD COCK-ROACH, immature specimen.

Center panel: HUNTING SPIDER. GOLDEN EYES, *Chrysopa*. HUNTING SPIDER.

Right panel: ORB WEAVER SPIDER (dorsal view). ORB WEAVER SPIDER (ventral view). HUNTING SPIDER.

BEE.   SCAVENGER BEETLE.   SPIDER (Net Weaver?).   BEE.

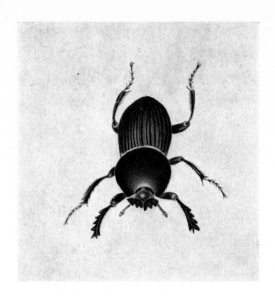

BEETLE.

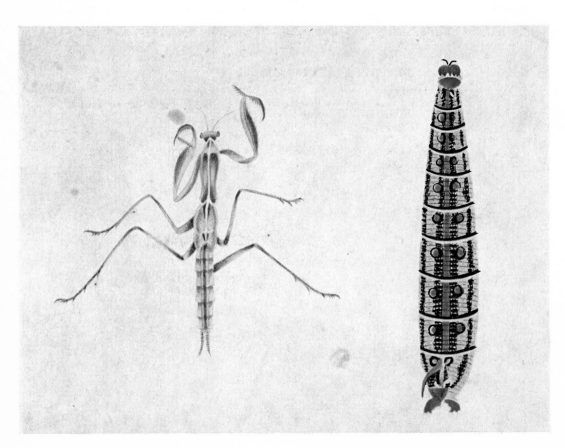

PRAYING MANTIS, immature.   SPHINX MOTH LARVA.

cut out his teaching almost altogether. This of course led to his dismissal, but he managed to persuade Mrs. Pirrie to allow him and Joseph a few days more at Oakley for his ornithological studies.

On October 10, 1821, Audubon and Joseph, again looking like vagabonds, arrived in New Orleans by steamer. Once more the Pamar family came to the rescue; so, too, did a family named Dmitry. Within a fortnight the painter was congratulating himself not only on having accumulated the sum of forty-two dollars from teaching art, but on having sixty-two more drawings than when he left Cincinnati the year before. A new suit and haircut had also improved his morale. The addition of the name of Mrs. William Brand to his list of pupils increased his confidence and prestige to the point where he felt justified in hiking his tuition fees to the highest of any in the city.

Mr. Brand, a rich and prominent citizen, decided that his young son of an earlier marriage should also join the drawing class. Even with more pupils, Audubon's income fell short, by far, of his growing prestige as an artist. He was hard put to it to care for himself and Joseph, in addition to his family, to whom he would send drafts of money as frequently as he could. Lucy, accompanied by her two sons, had left Cincinnati to be near her sister, Mrs. Nicholas Berthoud—daughter-in-law of the former French marquis who once protected Audubon from an angry mob in Kentucky.

Audubon urged his wife to give up her teaching and join him, but she was loath to relinquish her security until her husband's lot was less mercurial. Her stern and depressed replies to his pleas to join him deeply grieved him; nevertheless he continued to write, imploring her to come. At last she consented; the family arrived in New Orleans by steamer late in December.

For a while their little cottage in Dauphine Street resounded with merriment in the evenings, having not only Joseph and the musical Audubons for its inhabitants but also an old flutist who played by day in the open markets. Audubon had known poor Matabon in Kentucky and made him welcome.

Although Audubon's journal for 1822 was destroyed, his story can be pieced together from other sources. The struggle to find new pupils and portrait sitters apparently proved unrewarding; the family was forced to leave Dauphine Street, going forth before spring in different directions. Audubon's drawing pupil, Mrs. Brand, offered Lucy a post as governess in her New Orleans mansion, permitting her sons to accompany her. Audubon, dispirited and in poor health, left with Joseph Mason for Natchez, where a wealthy merchant from Majorca engaged him to teach his daughter French and music as well as art. On a nearby plantation lived the Wailes, a family of enthusiastic nature lovers whom the painter and Joseph joined in many a bird hunt. Among the notable results of these excursions is the "Orchard Oriole" in the *Birds of America,* showing a nest brought to the painter by one of the Wailes. Audubon, devoted to the oriole, remarked in his biography of the bird that he had never, during this period, been without its delightfully melodious company for a day, from the time he set out down the Ohio from Cincinnati. At the Waile plantation he watched it dart about among "the pendulous branches of the lofty tulip-trees, and move gracefully up and down, seeking in the expanding leaves and opening blossoms the caterpillar and the green beetle." He represented the bird on a tulip-tree twig, cut on the acres of his hospitable hunting companions.

By mid-April, spring fever and a longing to reach the Arkansas head-waters stirred in him, and he set out for old Fort Arkansas by steamer. Failing to attach himself to an expedition, he was obliged to return to Natchez, where he took yet another teaching position, this time at Elizabeth Female Academy in the nearby village of Washington. Victor and John joined him, and he sent them to school in Natchez, Lucy remaining with the Brands in New Orleans. Before long the naturalist began to detest his confinement, which was seriously retarding his bird collecting. His ever increasing desire to see his work published was the natural accompaniment of a growing assurance as to his powers, wonderfully reflected in such portraits as the "Whip-poor-will," a detail from which is shown on page 85.

Chronically depressed, intensely anxious to complete his birds, Audubon quit the academy in June. Shortly afterward, however, he contracted yellow fever in Natchez. When the good Dr. William Provan, whose name figures significantly in the family affairs of this period, had nursed him back to health, he contritely began to teach in the local school which Victor and Johnny had been attending.

In July, Joseph Mason departed by steamboat for Cincinnati, earning his way by sketching the passengers on board. Audubon, saddened at their parting, sent the lad off with paper and chalk, and pressed into his hands the old rifle he had bought in Philadelphia back in 1805 when he had begun to study American birds in earnest.

Needing to raise funds after his illness, the artist copied Trumbull's dramatic oil, "General Montgomery Before Quebec." When it failed to find a purchaser, Dr. Provan hit upon the idea of raffling it off at ten dollars per ticket. The scheme succeeded and Audubon was once more in pocket. More than that, his ticket won the picture.

The ailing child of the Brands, which had become Lucy's charge immediately upon its birth, died in New Orleans, whereupon Lucy left for Natchez to join her sons and husband. Soon after her arrival, necessity led her to look about for employment, and she became the governess of the child of a local minister. So seldom were her wages met that after two months she felt obliged to resign. The Audubon family situation was again acute. Though the thoughts of the kind-hearted Dr. Provan were much taken up just then with a girl in Feliciana, he rose nobly to the occasion with cash for food, clothing, and drawing materials to see his needy friends past their crisis.

Far from dwindling under the strain of his unending burdens, Audubon's artistic ambitions grew apace. Lucy's belief in him had also grown rather than diminished, and she agreed with a visiting English naturalist that his goal should be a trip to England. There a suitable engraver and sufficient subscribers might well be found.

42

The year 1822 saw technical advances in Audubon's art. He began to paint an undercoat of water color beneath his pastels, to gain the magical softness of the feathers of his owls, whippoorwills, and their particular kin. Always with an eye to the future, he decided, during December, to learn the use of oils. An itinerant portraitist, John Stein, agreed to be his teacher, and Audubon's sons were chosen as his models.

The following February, Dr. Provan, on the point of marrying Miss Jane Percy of West Feliciana parish, persuaded her widowed mother to engage Audubon as art and dancing master to the family. Travelers to that Louisiana neighborhood may still hear rumors of his graceful minuet, not to mention his volatile temper, frequently turned upon awkward members of his class of belles and beaux who gathered at the Percy plantation.

The late Robert Percy of the British Royal Navy had settled near Bayou Sarah in 1802 when Spain was the ruler, had helped lead the revolt against Spain in 1810, and was one of the three high court heads of the short-lived republic of West Florida. When the Audubons and their sons were introduced at the family estate, Beech Woods, Percy had been dead just three years. Lucy's duties included, besides the teaching of the Percys, the instruction of several neighboring planters' children. Legends of her admirable service and endearing personality are still much alive among the descendants of her devoted pupils in Feliciana.

Audubon recorded that the country around Beech Woods meant fully as much to the progress of the *Birds* as had Oakley plantation not far away. That it also figured in the beauty of the sketchbook goes without saying. The delights and wonders of those luxuriant woods and rolling savannas made it seem to him that nothing could go wrong. But, after several months, the happy illusion ended in sharp reversal. Audubon had been requested to execute portraits of the Percy daughters. Upon their completion Mrs. Percy examined them, pointing out to the proud and sensitive artist that he had painted the cheeks of the young ladies to a sallowness that was rudely realistic and unbecoming. A heated argument ensued, and Audubon spoke out with rage so unsparing that even Lucy felt he went too far. The painter was summarily ordered off the plantation.

On reaching the village nearby he sent word to Beech Woods for Victor to join him. The pair set out by steamer for Natchez, Audubon wishing that he might have had the cash to head north for Louisville or Philadelphia to enter "mercantile pursuits." This time, however, Lucy, staying on at the Percys, refused to indulge his whims or appropriate the money.

In Natchez a wealthy lady took a fancy to a water-color sketch which Audubon had made of the city, and her interest seemed about to save the day when she commissioned him to paint a huge oil exactly like it. Just as the painting was completed, his benefactress died, and her heirs refused both the picture and payment of the promised three hundred dollars. After neglect in a store where it hung unpurchased for years, it finally found an honored place in the Natchez mansion, Melrose.

Following this unfortunate incident, George Towers Duncan, a chance acquaintance, invited Audubon and Victor as hunting and fishing guests on his large plantation, The Towers, outside Natchez. But the Audubons, soon after their arrival, fell ill with yellow fever. Lucy, summoned to nurse them, rushed by carriage with Johnny from West Feliciana. The mistress of Beech Woods, anxious for the return of her children's tutor, sent word for Lucy to come back with her husband and sons, adding that bygones would be bygones. This they did as soon as Audubon could travel. At the Percys' estate, where he managed to hold his tongue, he spent hour upon hour in the lush August woods, adding steadily to his bird collection. By September his health had returned and Lucy urged him to visit Philadelphia, where she felt that a showing of his handsome drawings might lead to their publication. She also decided that Victor should learn commerce with his merchant uncle in Shippingport, near Louisville, and that his father could take him there on his journey north.

Early October found the painter headed up the Mississippi with his elder son. But no change of scene failed to bring its hardships. When the steamer *Magnet* found the low waters of the Ohio impossible to enter, Audubon and Victor decided to continue north on foot. The naturalist's published episode, "A Tough Walk for a Youth," describes the rigors of their journey, which proved almost too severe a test of fourteen-year-old Victor's endurance.

Depositing the lad with his uncle, Audubon proceeded to shift for himself in Louisville. Still coolly received there as a ne'er-do-well, he nevertheless managed to eke out an existence through the winter, decorating steamboat interiors with landscapes, painting shop signs, and doing any small job that came his way. Spring found him ready to face his destiny in Philadelphia. In April, 1824, short of funds and wholly without prospects, he arrived in the City of Brotherly Love.

III

OF INSECTS

Audubon and Pioneer Science

VISIONS—some lovely, others baneful—arise from the word *insect,* meaning six-legged creature. And the word for the study itself, *entomology,* does little to attract the ear and eye to the study of these most numerous of all animals of creation. Yet above, beneath, and within these mere designations lies a hidden universe of beauty, multitudinous activity, and divine design.

The struggles, handicaps, and perseverance of our early entomologists are, by themselves, as dramatic as the fascinating life processes of the creatures they investigated. These gentlemen, ironically enough, are almost all complete strangers to the public. Rare is the American schoolchild who cannot simply describe a butterfly's life span—from egg and caterpillar to pupa and adult. But few know the name of Thomas Say or his contemporaries, most of whom were friends of Audubon. The bird painter's relation to scientists who furthered the study of insects here and abroad has never before been appraised. Neither has the painted and written evidence of his interest been brought into the light for scrutiny. Until recently, when his paintings of mammals were revived, his fame rested primarily on his delineations of bird life.

One must go back to 1806 for the real birth of American entomology. The first important publication on insects was a quaint little pamphlet which today fetches about a hundred and fifty dollars on the market. *A Catalogue of Insects of Pennsylvania,* hardly more than a listing of 1,363 specimens by "Fred Val. Melsheimer, Minister of the Gospel," was printed in the village of York, Hanover County, Pennsylvania, in 1806. The preface, its only text, advanced rather homely ideas with what seems an acute sense of isolation, and without confidence that this publication was actually the first of its kind. The pamphlet reflects, almost touchingly, the primitive state of American entomological studies at the time. Not only for their rarity but for their charmingly antique literary cadence, his words earn the compliment of revival:

"I hereby offer to the Friends of Natural History a Catalogue of Insects, in the Collection of which I have spent my Hours of Recreation for some Years past. To the best of my Knowledge, I have but few predecessors in the United States in this Undertaking. For this Reason I may calculate on the Indulgence of the experienced Naturalist; in case some slight Errors should be found in it. It is an undeniable fact that Entomology has been considerably extended by American Insects; but yet there are many non-descript Genera and Species, to be met with by an observant Naturalist, which fully repay the Trouble of his Exertions. Hence arise the urgent Requests, and Invitations of European Naturalists; hence the ardent Desire to possess American insects: and this is likewise the strongest Excitement for American Entomologists to make themselves more intimately acquainted with the Productions of their country. Should the present Undertaking meet the Approbation of the Friends of Natural History in the United States, then this Catalogue will be continued from Time to Time . . ."

The introduction continues with a brief invitation to readers to exchange insects which the Reverend Mr. Melsheimer lacked for others which he could provide. "Should there be any Friends of natural history who would wish for a collection of Insects, I am inclined to supply them with one subject of each Species at the Rate of Five Dollars per hundred." In classifying insects as he found them, he tried to keep to the system of Fabricius, also acknowledging the help of one "Professor Knock" of Brunswick, Germany, with whom he corresponded. "Part the First" was the beginning and end of Melsheimer's published labors, though he closed his remarks on a hopeful note: "With pleasure I should have made some observations on, and given a short description of, some of the more important subjects, if time and other occupations had permitted."

Melsheimer published no illustrations. Only the Englishman, Mark Catesby, had previously shown any of our insects, which he did in *The Natural History of Carolina, the Floridas, and the Bahama Islands* (1731-1743). Melsheimer made no mention of W. D. Peck, Harvard professor whose articles on New England insects began to appear in 1795.

Eleven years later the first formal if frustrated attempt to publish a book on our insects was made by Thomas Say in 1817. The thirty-year-old naturalist, a Philadelphia Quaker, referred to Melsheimer as "the parent of American entomology." Posterity, however, has conferred that honor upon Say, author of about a hundred writings on science. The York clergyman might rather be considered the father of *Pennsylvania* insect study. Thomas Say, though he entered the limelight with a book on shells, more than earned his title. Those with even a slight knowledge of Audubon's writings on birds and mammals will need no reminder as to his familiarity with the works of Say who, for the pioneer era, knew a great deal about all branches of the animal kingdom.

In the activities of Audubon and Say there are, in fact, noteworthy parallels, even as to insects. The difference is that Audubon never made them a specific avenue of study, but only as they figured in the varied diet of his birds. In order to bring tentative order out of confusion and uncertainty, Say had to confess his own and his country's comparative ignorance of entomology. He is perhaps as much the hero for that as for his *American Entomology*, issued between 1824 and 1828 in three volumes.

The first number of the first volume of Say's work appeared in 1817— a mere folder of six colored engravings with a preface which, in a limited way, is a pioneer science classic. Sparse as to facts, it nevertheless makes engaging reading, with its gentle philosophizing, moralizing, and color.

Say's first taste of prominence came from his ancestry rather than his scholarship. When he was approaching young manhood, Pennsylvanians were still discussing his grandfather's vision in which the old Quaker, in a trance, is supposed to have visited heaven. Say's father Benjamin, an apothecary and physician, published an account of this supernatural occurrence. His people also figured in Penn's colonization of "Sylvania."

Say's boyhood preoccupation with butterflies and beetles, much to his father's disappointment, eventually led him to come to grips with the systematic orders and to desert pharmacy altogether. At twenty-five he was elected a founding member of Philadelphia's Academy of Natural Sciences. To practice what his idol Seneca had preached about simple living, he subsisted mostly on bread and milk, relieved by only an occasional chop or egg. Six to twelve cents was his daily budget. He often insisted that he wished he might have been made with a hole in his side where a little food to keep him going might be stored.

In 1816 Say began work on his first publication; but, after the initial issue in 1817, there was a lull until 1824. The first romantic cover design is a far cry from the sober equivalents of modern times, showing two cupids in pursuit of insects. The title page, no less bucolic, represents a scene in a glade with small fauna creeping busily about. But Say's work was an auspicious beginning. Charles Alexandre Lesueur, French naturalist who spent some important years in this country, was responsible for these fanciful embellishments as well as for some of the insect plates. His title page design shared honors with this poetic effusion from Stillingfleet:

"Each moss,
Each shell, each crawling insect, holds a rank
Important in the plan of Him who fram'd
This scale of beings."

The preface by Say is a veritable essay on the prevailing state of the study of entomology, a promising hint of American works to come.

"But little, I might almost say nothing," wrote Say, "has yet been done in the United States in relation to the very interesting and important science upon which this work is intended to treat. While, in other departments of natural history, we have publications honourable to the republic, there is not, as far as I know, in the archives of American science, the record of an indigenous work on this subject."

Say turned to the state of things abroad: "In Europe, a celebrated writer informs us, the insects—so numerous, so diversified in their characters, in their colouring so elegant and varied, and so singular in their manners— have so much interest that, of all the animals, they have been the most observed and the most studied; and they are those on which the labours of naturalists have been the most exercised.

"But in the United States, entomology, of all sciences, has been regarded with the least attention by the learned. . . . With us . . . many votaries . . .

choose those departments where knowledge is more readily acquired, and where the labour . . . is not arduous or protracted. Entomology, although captivating at a distance, [has] at its threshold . . . so many difficulties that the beholder is deterred from prosecuting his researches. The variety of systems, the obscurity of the distinctive characteristics [of insects], and often the great requisite nicety of discrimination upon which some of these systems are founded, the want of a guide such as would be afforded by good books of plates—all conspire to retard the progress of the student. . . . We may also add the difficulty of procuring the many splendid and costly works of European authors, our booksellers being unwilling to incur the risk of importing them unless expressly ordered. Attributable to these causes is the absence of knowledge of this science and of taste for its cultivation." Here Say injected a note of impatience with his benighted and indifferent fellows:

"Indeed there are not wanting among the uninformed, individuals who harbor the almost impious opinion that insects are despicable because they are minute, and that the study of them is little better than contemptible, trifling, and prodigality of time. This opinion is too unphilosophical to deserve notice, or serious reply. It is impious, inasmuch as it assumes that a portion of the labours of the Creator, which we are informed he contemplated with pleasure, and in his wisdom pronounced good, are altogether futile and of a nature too trifling for the serious attention of man.

"Much might be said in opposition to this absurd notion, the offspring of ignorance, and enough has been said by numerous authors . . . to entitle the claim of these minute but most formidable of all animals to an exalted rank in our respect and consideration."

Say lamented that Europeans were at the moment "infinitely better acquainted" with our American insects than we were, as their publications clearly demonstrated. He said that he felt regret as a diligent zoologist "that no one arose among us to investigate and describe" additional species. "I was anxious in vain that some of my countrymen, whose talents and scientific acquirements were greater than my own and more adequate to the task, would make known to the world this Protean people. At length, urged exclusively by a love for the pursuit, I have undertaken this work, though not without considerable hesitation . . . acting the part of a pioneer in an untried path—destitute of a colleague with whom to consult in case of doubt—without extensive and well arranged cabinets, and with but few books for reference. I am constrained to rely solely on my own exertions."

T. W. Harris was one American whom Say might well have praised. In 1823 Harris brought out the first of a series of papers on economic entomology, which led to the first book on the subject in 1841, for which he received $175 from the state of Massachusetts.

Like Melsheimer, Say invited help and correspondence. He expressed obligation to Donovan, author of the *Natural History of British Insects,* and to Latreille's improved Linnaean method of classification. He promised "truth" only, the best of plates, a glossary, and no "injudicious multiplication of species." Then he closed: "With these prefatory observations I take leave of the first number of American Entomology, yet not without solicitude for its fate. But a full ray of hope enlivens the future."

Eight insects were admirably executed in natural color on six plates by Titian Peale and others. Say himself was not an artist. Against five of the plates were symbols pointing to this bewildered footnote: "Those with asterisks prefixed are supposed to be new." No real text and no glossary went with it, but only a preface full of apologies, hopes, and promises, few of which would be fulfilled despite Say's gallant and persevering efforts. Seven years later, in 1824, Thomas Say resumed publication in New Harmony, Indiana, where he went with other leading scientists of his city on Robert Owen's famous "boatload of knowledge." Bound down the Ohio for a socialist "paradise," the group was doomed to speedy failure.

Say's deference to the scholars of Europe piques our curiosity, and a glance at Old World activity which inspired his own efforts illumines the whole panorama of entomology.

Long before Aristotle, that Greek genius of the fourth century B.C., mankind had, in its way, taken cognizance of insects. The scarab beetle dominated the entire social scene of the ancient Egyptians, now forming a hieroglyph or language character, now symbolizing the globe of the sun. The creature was used with symbolic significance in tomb engravings based on the Book of the Dead. One scarab of granite from Heliopolis, sacred to the sun god, is of colossal size. Some decorative scarabs have rams' heads; others appear on ornaments and sealstones, occasionally bearing mottoes. A few mummified beetles have also been found in ancient Egyptian tombs.

Hebrew scripture abounds in allusions to bees, ants, and locusts. But Middle Eastern peoples were not properly inquisitive about insects, except to note their effect on agriculture and to attribute to them superstitious meanings. Ages of such uninquiring indifference passed before Aristotle began his brilliant researches, collecting and dissecting animals, including insects—and separating crustaceans from the latter. His systems, devised for animals generally, were regarded as adequate by scientists for almost two thousand years, until fresh strides were taken by European investigators.

The study of entomology progressed from the structure and life history of insects to anatomy and development, to systematic classification and interrelationship, to habits and life relations, and finally to the study of fossils.

The seventeenth and eighteenth centuries saw notable advances. In 1651 Harvey revived Aristotle and voiced certain new theories later to be disproved by Swammerdam. In 1668 the Italian, Redi, wrote on the maggot and the impossibility of its spontaneous generation from the matter of its haunts. Malpighi's treatise on the silkworm, published in 1669, still ranks as a classic. J. Swammerdam's *Biblia Naturae*, dated 1737 but written at least half a century earlier, described the life history of various insects. In England, 1705 marked the year that John Ray's study of the metamorphosis, or life stages, of insects was published. In a limited sense Ray's interest in altering the outmoded classifications of the past makes him a forerunner of Linnaeus, whose immortal *Systems of Nature* (1735) included a chapter on insects.

Linnaeus divided the insects into orders which, to the present day, prevail: beetles; flies; butterflies and moths; caddisflies; nerve-winged insects; scorpionflies; bees, wasps, and ants.

In Denmark, J. C. Fabricius carried on work in the Linnaean system, publishing his findings in 1775. In France J. B. Lamarck carried the same system forward with a publication in 1801; and in 1800-1805 Baron Cuvier's *Lessons in Comparative Anatomy* made him the founder of this branch of research. W. E. Leach, leader of Linnaeus' disciples in England, made his worthy, published contribution in 1815.

Also important were the life histories of the insects written by De Réaumur in France, De Geer in Sweden, and Roesel in Germany, working in the eighteenth century. A fuller accounting of this period would include other names, deserving but less illustrious.

It may come as a surprise to some that none of the national entomological societies of Europe were formed until a dozen years after Audubon painted the insects of his sketchbook, and until Say had brought out his famous work in 1824-1828. The first such American group was the Entomological Society of Philadelphia, founded in 1859, eight years after Audubon's death and a quarter of a century after Say's.

Nature lovers who find the beauty of Audubon's sketchbook its chief attraction will feel a bond of sympathy with the much misunderstood and maligned "Aurelians" who flourished in the days before Linnaeus, whose methods of study brought them down to earth. They collected butterflies and other lovely six-legged creatures without concern for their scientific rank. This directionless collecting mania might be likened to the pressing of flowers merely to preserve their evanescent charms. The Aurelians were innocent of serious motives, and were consequently regarded as harmless lunatics by those who did not share their lightly aesthetic motives. The spectacle of a butterfly net in the hands of a wild-eyed and breathless rambler has oftentimes, in fact, been made ridiculous by illustrators of the last two centuries. Simple butterfly collectors, possibly descended from the outcast Aurelian tradition, have long filled one corridor of mankind's stock gallery of eccentrics. Many such net wielder has figured in mystery fiction. The madman or simpleton, of course, is none other than the villain in disguise.

The virtual absence of entomological research in our own early days is made painfully apparent by a memoir of Say written by George Ord of the Philadelphia Academy in 1859 for a complete edition of Say's works:

"At the date of Mr. Say's induction into this temple of science," wrote Ord, referring to the Academy's beginnings with mixed irony and affection, "the whole collection consisted of some half a dozen common insects, a few madrepores and shells, a dried toad fish and a stuffed monkey . . . calculated rather to excite merriment than to procure respect, but, in the end, the nucleus of one of the most beautiful and valuable collections in the United States. . . . The founders had anything in view but the advancement of science. Strange as it may appear, it is nevertheless true that the club of humorists which subsequently dignified the association under the imposing title of Academy, held its weekly meetings merely for the purpose of amusement, confining itself to those objects which would be most conducive to that end. . . . A higher object was suggested to the attention of the association in the process of time . . . to awaken public curiosity, and thereby gain members, and the means for collecting and preserving natural curiosities. At the date of Mr. Say's joining the Society, this plan had been recently adopted."

In the complete edition of Say which was brought out the same year as the founding of the first American entomological society in his city, Ord spoke with the tone of a veteran of science musing nostalgically on the backward past.

Figuring in Say's history is Alexander Wilson, the Scottish-born "father of American ornithology," who met Audubon in Henderson, Kentucky, in 1810 and showed the painter his own drawings of birds. Wilson's promise of help to Say temporarily offset the latter's discouragement at the beginning of his gallant project, but Wilson died in 1813 before he could make good that offer.

In 1818 Say joined an expedition to the Georgia and Florida coasts, the latter of which was then under Spain, but Indian hostility quickly forced his party out. The following year he went with the Major Stephen H. Long expedition to the West as zoologist, a project of such importance in American frontier history that no account of the westward movement is complete without it. The name of Titian Ramsay Peale (1799-1885), son of the eminent painter Charles Willson Peale, and brother of Rembrandt and Raphael Peale who also made names for themselves as artists and associates of the Peale Museum, has never received proper recognition. Titian Peale's name appears in few if any biographical dictionaries of his century. Peale, Say's assistant on the expedition, helped collect and delineate animals, but the official artist was an Englishman named Samuel Seymour, whose Indian and Western scenes are well known to Americana collectors.

Peale was to execute twenty-six drawings of insects for Say's *American Entomology* on his return from the West.[1] With Say he was soon to meet Audubon in Cincinnati. And he would encounter him auspiciously again in Philadelphia, while illustrating the continuation of Wilson's work on American birds by Charles Lucien Bonaparte, nephew of Napoleon.

The Major Long expedition set sail from Pittsburgh in May, 1819, amid cannon salutes and waving crowds on the Allegheny shores. Its members, including Say and Peale, were in high spirits. They could not foresee the illness, Indian troubles, river perils, stark privation, and other trials that lay ahead. Peale's little-known journal describes their craft:

"She draws about two feet and a half water, the wheels placed in the stern in order to avoid trees, snags and sawyers. On the quarter deck is a bullet-proof house for the steersman. On the right hand wheel is *James Monroe* in capital letters; and on the left, *J. C. Calhoun,* they being the two propelling powers of the expedition. She has a mast to ship and unship

1 Examples of Peale's work appear on pages 88 and 89.

at pleasure, which carries a square and topsail. On the bow is carved the figure of a large serpent, through the gapping mouth of which the waste steam issues. It will give to the Indians an idea that the boat is pulled along by this monster. Our arms consist of one brass four pounder mounted on the bow, four brass 2⅞-inch howitzers, two on swivels, and two on field carriages, two wolf pieces carrying four ounce balls; twelve muskets, six rifles, and several fowling pieces, an air gun, twelve sabers, pistols, and a quantity of private arms of various sorts and ammunition. . . . A commissioner of the Bible Society gave us two bibles and one or two other books for the good of our souls, and to remind us in the wilderness that we carry the prejudice of ——."

At stops to gather wood for fueling the boat the expedition attracted "universal attention" from settlers, squatters, Indians, and folk of smaller craft who came alongside. They reached Cincinnati on May 9, the seventh day after they left Pittsburgh.

Audubon missed the expedition on the outward journey, but he was in Cincinnati at the time of their return from the Rockies, a year later. It is regrettable that only half of Peale's journal remains, not merely because it must have contained the expedition's impressions of Audubon and his drawings, but because the portion that survived is stimulating fare.

When the Long expedition steamed down the Ohio past Henderson, Audubon, then living there, doubtless knew nothing of it. He was deep in the throes of business troubles, briefly mentioned in the first chapter. His "infernal mill," as he called it, had dragged him into debt, and one crisis precipitated another. One day, in an altercation over some transaction, he stabbed a man in self-defense. As Audubon lay at home half-conscious from the injuries his adversary had inflicted, an angry mob of rival sympathizers stormed his gate to administer a whipping. Luckily, Audubon's relative by marriage, James Berthoud, an *émigré* from the French Revolution, kept them from meting out frontier justice. The courage and calm of the white-headed former Marquis de St. Pierre, husband of a one-time lady-in-waiting to Marie Antoinette, held back the would-be assailants.

About this time, to make matters worse, Lucy's brother, Tom Bakewell, withdrew as Audubon's partner, taking his financial investment with him. Rapidly following on that reversal was Audubon's controversy with an immigrant brother of the English poet Keats. George Keats had recently arrived in Henderson to seek his fortune, his family accepting the Audubons' hospitality for a time. Keats was now claiming that the painter had defaulted on the sale to him of a river boat, the craft in question having sunk, cargo and all, in the Ohio. A succession of calamities followed for Audubon: the failure of the local bank, the loss of his mill, his home, his acres, of all, indeed, but the clothing on his back, his drawings, and his gun!

Despondent and almost without hope, he walked to Louisville, where, far from finding solace, he was at once arrested by his creditors and thrown into jail. A newly passed law relating to solvency happily effected his swift release. Lucy and the boys joined him in Louisville, and they managed to live for a while on what he could earn through chalk portrait commissions.

Later he recalled that only his frequent retreats to the Kentucky woods and their birds saved him from utter despair.

Within the year Audubon was off to Cincinnati, hoping that fortune now might smile on him. The prospect of his new post at the Western Museum, where he was to officiate as taxidermist, temporarily buoyed his spirits. But his brief meeting with the members of the returning Long expedition was one of the few memories of Cincinnati that he cherished. "Well do I recollect how Major Long, T. Peale, Thomas Say and others stared at my drawings of birds at the time," he wrote in "Myself," his auto-biography. This initial meeting with Say and Peale strengthened his long-ing to explore the Rockies, an ambition which never left him though the nearest he came to its fulfillment was the Montana border in 1843, during an expedition for the *Quadrupeds*, his second great project.

If his conversation in Cincinnati with these men touched upon insects —and it seems likely that it may have done so (for no report of Say's vicissi-tudes would be complete without them)—Audubon must have learned of Say's projected book. He may even have seen some of Peale's sketches for *American Entomology*. One account of the expedition states that "notes referring to grasshoppers and to many other insects collected on the Platte and about the mountains were subsequently lost in the robbery committed by three of the soldiers, who deserted from the party in the country of the Osages." Doubtless Audubon heard of this, too.

Say's *American Entomology* offers many delightful, short period pieces of description, even if there is a relative dearth of new information. A sam-ple or two of the more colorful lines affords an idea. Opposite a fine en-graving of a walking stick drawn by Peale, Say remarked that it was caught "on the apron of a gig" and was the only specimen known to him. Speak-ing of a locust, he borrowed from the ancients:

"There seems little doubt that this species constituted one of the plagues of Egypt mentioned in the Bible (probably the *G. migratorius*), and that John the Baptist was compelled to use them for food during his sojourn in the wilderness. Many travellers assure us that they constitute an agree-able food. When fried with a little salt they have the taste of Cray-fish. Arabs preserve large quantities for winter consumption."

Another of the walking sticks evoked from Say this fascinating homily:

"We are told that there was a time when a piece of wood was trans-formed into a serpent, and even in the present age of knowledge, a hair fallen from the mane or tail of a horse into a stream of water is believed by many to become animated into a distinct being. Dead leaves shed by the parent tree are said to change gradually into animals of singular shape, and to have changed their place of abode under the eye of the historians who related the wonderful tale. Dead sticks also were said to sprout legs, to move from place to place, and perform all the functions of a living body.

"These, and a thousand other equally ridiculous tales, were at one period or another more or less generally admitted as indisputable truths, and to contradict them would only be to expose oneself to the imputation of ignorance or criminal faithlessness. And although at present the possibility of making a living serpent out of wood, and the story of animated leaves and sticks would be despised as absurd, yet many are to be found, both in Europe and America, who firmly believe in the reanimation of a horsehair. But the most obvious errors have often a shadow of truth whereon to rest, or palliate, if not excuse them by the plea of ignorance or mistake.

"The historian of the walking leaf may have been deceived by the *Mantis siccifolium* of Linnaeus, the wings of which have some resemblance to a leaf. The Gordius resembles a horsehair, and no doubt gave rise to the story of the metamorphosis above mentioned. The account of the walking sticks may have very honestly originated from the singular appearance and form of some insect of the present genus. These are long, slender and cylindrical; and on a first view it is not a little difficult to reconcile their appearance to our preconceived ideas of the general insect form. They are nevertheless perfectly inoffensive, and feed altogether on vegetables. They are probably indebted for safety from the attacks of their enemies, the birds, to their deceptive appearance, and by their general similarity in point of color to the object on which they rest."

Beside Peale's beautiful "Trojan" butterfly, Say wrote colorfully of his experiments with the theory of pain in insects. "Much has been said and written relative to the acuteness of the sensation of pain in insects. Whatever may have a tendency to prevent acts of wanton barbarity ought certainly to be encouraged as far as it is conformable to truth, but not further. The poet's assertion that the worm, crushed beneath the foot of the passenger, 'feels a pang as great as when a giant dies,' cannot be substantiated. It proves nothing but that the author declared positively what he merely believed or imagined to be true. My opinion, to the contrary of all this, is founded on such facts as the following. I caught an insect belonging to the present genus, and having impaled it by passing a pin vertically through its body it escaped from my hand. The pin being light, and no injurious pressure having been exerted on its body, the insect flew to a flower, apparently with its usual facility. Unrolling its elongated proboscis, it proceeded to extract the sweet fluid from the nectar, as if no mortal wound had been inflicted."

Say's remarks on the "Pompilus," of which Peale drew a fine illustration, would do credit to a nature book of any period: ". . . Descending the Arkansas river with Major Long's party, I was one day surprised to see a species of this genus, dragging along the ground the body of the gigantic bird-catching spider." But where Say thinks of "intelligence" as somehow synonymous with instinct, his ideas would now most likely be challenged: "In the present order of insects called Hymenoptera [bees, wasps, and ants] by Linnaeus, are many species whose manners are highly interesting. Living together harmoniously in large communities, and laboring for the attainment of a common object, such species exhibit such eminent proofs of intelligence as to stagger the vain theorist in the midst of his speculations, and to render insecure the distinction which he has endeavored to establish between the blindness of instinct and the splendid nature of reason." He

54

was referring to the species philanthus, and explained that the large word was a compound of the Greek for "I love a flower."

These excerpts are not in any way presented to belittle Say's accomplishments, for he is, and will always be, remembered for his notable pioneering efforts and unswerving integrity. They are included solely to suggest the relatively backward state of one branch of science in our country at the time when Audubon's sketchbook, with its insects, was created.

Insect details may be seen in many of Audubon's early drawings of the birds, notably those at the Houghton Library of Harvard University. One drawing that he made in 1805 while on a visit to France shows a woodpecker with its prey. Another sketch from his early American period, "Crested Flycatcher," includes the nest of a hornet. A woodpecker that he drew in Henderson in 1814 is seen eying a company of beetles which it has just flushed with its bill from beneath the bark. "Bartram's Sandpiper," an engaging early work, has caught a worm. Around the bill of the "Willett," a drawing dated May 8, 1815, a plump earthworm is intricately entwined.

Insects were of vital assistance to Audubon in his determination to show birds in "animated" attitudes—true to life. The winged brethren, when about their business, are of course largely on the lookout for insects. In his portraits of birds he took care, from the very beginning of his work, to include beetles, caterpillars, worms, spiders, flies, and other natural quarry. His essay on his method of drawing makes absorbing reading, no less so where it touches on insects and reptiles as bird fare:

"When, as a little lad, I first began my attempts at representing birds on paper, I was far from possessing much knowledge of their nature . . . and oh! what bills and claws I did draw, to say nothing of a perfectly straight line for a back, and a tail stuck in anyhow, like an unshipped rudder. My father constantly impressed on me that nothing in the world possessing life and animation was easy to imitate. He hoped as I grew older I would become more and more alive to this. He was so kind to me . . . his words became my law.

"My first drawings were European specimens, represented in stiff unmeaning profiles. My next set was begun in America, where I drew specimens hung by a string tied to one foot, to show every portion as the wings lay loosely spread. In this manner I made some pretty fair signs for poulterers.

"One day while watching the habits of a pair of Pewees at Mill Grove, a thought struck my mind like a flash of light . . . a desire to represent nature in her own way, alive and moving! I formed literally hundreds of outlines of my favorites, the Pewees . . . and fancied I had mounted a step on the high pinnacle before me. For months together, I outlined birds as I observed them, either alighted or on the wing . . . A second thought came to my assistance. By means of threads I raised or lowered a head, wing, or tail; yet much was wanting. When I saw the living birds, I felt the blood rush to my temples, and almost in despair I spent about a month without drawing, but in deep thought.

"I had drawn from the 'manikin' whilst a pupil of Jacques Louis David in Paris, so I cogitated on how far a manikin of a bird would answer. I labored with wood, cork, and wires, and formed a grotesque figure—a tolerable-looking Dodo. A friend roused my ire by laughing. . . . I gave it a kick, broke it to atoms, walked off, and thought again.

"I frequently dreamed that I had made a new discovery. Long before day, one morning, I leaped out of bed, ordered a horse to be saddled, and went off at a gallop to the little village of Norristown, five miles distant. Not a door was open there, for it was not yet daylight. I went to the river, took a bath, returned to town, entered the first open shop, bought some wire of different sizes, and leaped on my steed again. The wife of my tenant, I really believe, thought that I was mad, as I told her I only wanted my gun when she offered me breakfast. I was off to the creek, shot the first Kingfisher I met, carried it home by the bill, sent for the miller, and bade him bring me a piece of board of soft wood. I began filing sharp points to some pieces of wire, pierced the body of the fishing bird and fixed it on the board . . . in a pretty fair attitude. The last wire elevated the bird's tail delightfully—there stood before me the *real* Kingfisher. I outlined it, aided by compasses and my eyes, colored it, finished it, without a thought of hunger. My honest miller stood by, the while, delighted to see me pleased. This was what I shall call my first drawing actually from nature."

All his life Audubon carried La Fontaine's writings, turning often to the fable which admonishes: "He who sees a great deal will have much to remember." He said that to him this meant he was to study nature and observe all he could, for the sake of his work. Continuing with his essay, "My Style of Drawing Birds," he explained further:

"I gradually became acquainted with their forms and habits. . . . The Pewees, I knew, were positively fly-catchers. This led me to the discovery that every bird truly of that genus, when standing, was usually in a passive attitude. They sat upright, now and then glancing upwards or sideways to watch the approach of their insect prey. If in pursuit of this prey, their movements through the air were the same. . . . Amongst the water birds also I found characteristic manners. . . . The more I understood all these particulars, the better representations I made of the originals."

Bird and Insect Dramas

Each bird that Audubon brought home he examined for evidence of diet. Not only his text for the *Birds of America* but his notebooks and diaries abound in minute data, so that the feeding habits of the flycatchers, beetle-eaters, and the rest might be accurately represented in pictures with their prey and fully accounted for in his biographies of the species. In the latter are long passages describing the search for food—veritable bird and insect dramas. So detailed and vivid are the biographies—even though cer-

BLUEBIRDS with caterpillar of the TUSSOCK MOTH. Painted at Beech Woods, 1821. (Detail from the *Birds* folio.)

57

YELLOW-BREASTED CHAT feeding young.
(Detail from the *Birds* folio.)

(Photo: Cooper Union Museum)

58

ROBIN feeding caterpillar of TUSSOCK MOTH to young. (Detail from the *Birds* folio).

(Facsimile detail from the *Birds* folio.)

RUBY-THROATED HUMMINGBIRD. Painted at Beech Woods, 1825.

Opposite page: COLUMBIAN HUMMINGBIRD (ANNA'S). The floral details for these insectlike birds by Audubon were painted by Maria Martin for the *Birds* folio. (See page 81.)

UPLAND PLOVER and ICHNEUMON FLY, *Ophion Macrurum*. (Facsimile detail from the *Birds* fo

FRINGILLID and SPIDER, *Theridion*. (Facsimile.) Plant and spider by Maria Martin. For the *Birds*

(Photos: Cooper Union Museum)

NIGHTHAWK and BEETLES. Upper beetle is identified as *Pelidnota punctata*. Painted in New Orleans or Natchez region, c. 1822. (Facsimile detail from *Birds* folio.)

Top left: HOP MERCHANT BUTTERFLY, *Polygonia comma*, by Maria Martin for Audubon's GROSBEAKS. *Top right*: FISH FLY, *Chauliodes*, in the "Gullbilled Tern" plate. *Right*: UNDERWING MOTH, *Catocala*, in the "Trumpeter Swan" plate. *Below*: TYRANT FLYCATCHER and FLESH FLIES. All illustrations from Audubon's *Birds* folio. The three upper illustrations are facsimile size.

YELLOW-THROATED VIREO with WASP, *Elis five-cincta*. Insect and plant by Joseph Mason. Painted at Oakley, 1821. (Facsimile detail from the *Birds* folio.)

Details from the
Birds folio.

BLACK-BILLED CUCKOO and BEE FLY. Plant and bee fly by Joseph Mason for Audubon's bird.

AMERICAN REDSTART and PAPER WASPS, *Polistes*. Painted at Oakley, 1821.

(Photos: Cooper Union Museum)

WALLOW-TAILED KITE with GARTER SNAKE. Painted at Oakley, 1821. (From the *Birds* folio.)

GREEN HERON with LUNA MOTH, *Actias luna*. (Facsimile detail from the *Birds* folio.)

68

tain particulars may be open to question—that they rank with the finest of nature writing. For full appreciation of his insect and bird renderings as art generated by the love of nature, one would do well also to read his writings. Only then is it possible to grasp that passion which begot his immortal linear impressions.

Turn for instance to his Mississippi kite which has just landed on a branch with a beetle in its grasp. Then hear this account, enriched by delectable scenic details:

"When numberless insects, cramped in their hanging shells, are impatiently waiting for the full expansion of their wings, when the vernal flowers swell their bursting leaflets, and the rich-leaved magnolia opens its pure blossoms to the Humming-bird, then look up, and you will see the Mississippi Kite sailing over the scene. He glances towards the earth with his fiery eye, sweeps along, now with the gentle breeze, now against it, and seizes here and there the high-flying giddy bug and allays his hunger. Suddenly he spies some creeping thing that changes like the chameleon from vivid green to dull brown, to escape his notice. It is the red-throated panting lizard that has made its way to the highest branch of a tree in quest of food. It remains motionless, so well does it know the prowess of the bird of prey, but its caution is vain and its fate is sealed.

"The Kite arrives in Lower Louisiana about mid-April, keeping to the borders of the woods. At times it floats in the air as if motionless, or in broad regular circles, then it slides along again before renewing its curves. With the swiftness of an arrow it passes almost within touching distance of a branch where it has seen a small lizard or an insect, then it may ascend again, disappointed. Again it is observed flying round a tree trunk to secure large insects, sweeping with astonishing velocity. When pursuing a large insect or small reptile, it turns its body sidewise, throws out its legs, expands its talons, and generally seizes its prey in an instant, feeding on the wing with as much ease as on a tree branch."

During his residence at Oakley plantation in Louisiana, Audubon painted his remarkable "Swallow-tailed Hawk" [Kite], illustrated on page 67. So precise, compact, and emblematic in conception is this portrait of a bird in flight, with a writhing garter snake in its talons, that the effect is more decoratively art-conscious than most of his works. The animation is more than suspended; it is frozen to perhaps excessive design perfection. But what a miraculous transition it represents from his earlier, less consciously aspiring portraits of birds. To elucidate the wild and arresting portrait of the kite he wrote:

"The flight of this elegant species of Hawk is singularly beautiful and protracted. . . . They always feed on the wing, soaring to an immense height, pursuing the large insects called *Musquito Hawks,* and performing the most singular evolutions imaginable, using their tail with elegance of motion. They sweep close over the fields, sometimes seeming to alight for a moment to secure a snake, and holding it fast by the neck, carry it off, and devour it in the air. When they are searching for grasshoppers and caterpillars it is not difficult to approach them under a cover of a fence or a tree. A whole flock will come over one dead hawk among them as if intent on carrying it off."

Audubon was never content to choose his models from woods and fields. His plate in the *Birds* purporting to show three lively sparrow hawks is actually but one model, his pet hawk Nero, whom one finds engaging, if a trifle intimidating, in the following description: "No bird can be more easily raised and kept than this beautiful Hawk. I once found a young male that had dropped from the nest before it was able to fly. Its cries for food attracted my notice, and I discovered it lying near a log. It was large, and covered with soft white down through which the young feathers protruded. Its little blue bill and yet grey eyes made it look not unlike an owl. I took it home and named it Nero. In a few weeks it grew very beautiful, and became so voracious that I turned it out to see how it would shift for itself. It soon hunted for grasshoppers and other insects. On returning from my walks I now and then threw a dead bird high in the air, and the young Hawk never failed to perceive it, sometimes catching it before it reached the ground. The little fellow attracted the notice of his brothers, living hard by, who, accompanied by their parents, at first gave it chase, and forced it to take refuge behind one of the window shutters, where it usually passed the night. Soon it became gentler towards us, as if forgiving its desertion. My bird was fastidious in its choice of food. . . . To the last he continued kind to me, and never failed to return at night to his favorite roost behind the window shutter. His courageous disposition often amused the family. He would sail off from his stand and pursue a tame duck, which, setting up a loud quack, would waddle off in great alarm with the Hawk sticking to her. But as often happens to adventurers of similar spirit, his audacity cost him his life. A hen and her brood chanced to attract his notice, but this hen's parental affection inspired her with a courage greater than his own. The conflict, a severe one, ended the adventures of poor Nero."

On nights of bright moonlight Audubon would prowl the woods to watch the ways of the nocturnal creatures. In the opinion of this writer he has painted no more beautiful and *alive* an example than the bird he called the "Fairy of the Night," or chuck-will's-widow. Passages devoted to its description have moments of grandeur: "About the middle of March, the forests of Louisiana are heard to echo with the well-known notes of this interesting bird. No sooner has the sun disappeared, and the nocturnal insects emerged from their burrows, than the sounds, *'chuck-will's-widow,'* repeated with power and clarity six or seven times in as many seconds, strike the ear. They bring pleasure mingled with a certain melancholy. The sounds forebode a peaceful and calm night . . . By day they roost in tree hollows, where I have found them lodged in the company of bats, the birds asleep on the mouldering particles of the wood. When seized and brought to the light of day, they open and close their eyes as if it were painful to encounter so bright a light. They snap their bill and shuffle along to try and escape.

"At the approach of night this bird begins to sing, launches into the air and sweeps over cotton fields or sugar plantations, cutting all sorts of figures. It suddenly checks its course, inclines to the right or left, secures a beetle or a moth, continues its flight, passes and repasses hundreds of times over the same field, and now and then alights on a fence stake. It may be seen following a road or path on the wing, and picking up the beetle which is emerging from the ground, or it gives chase to the insects flying high in the air, perhaps on the passage of the insects from one wood to another. I have seen it poise itself on its wings opposite the trunk of a tree, and seize insects crawling on the bark. It inspects the whole tree with motions as light as those by which the Humming-bird flutters from one flower to another. In this manner the Chuck-will's-widow spends the greater part of the night. . . . This bird forms no nest. A little space is carelessly scratched among dead leaves, and in it the eggs, which are elliptical, dull olive in color, and speckled with brown, are dropped. Should you touch or handle these dear fruits of happy love, you would search in vain for them were you to return to the place later. For the bird perceives at once that they have been meddled with, and both parents remove them to some other part of the woods, just as they do with the young when very small. This singular occurrence has occupied my thoughts as much as the equally singular way in which the *Cow Bunting* deposits her eggs, putting them one by one in the nests of other birds of different species from her own, to be hatched by the latter. The removal is performed by the birds taking the eggs in their large mouth. [This testimony about the removal of the eggs by bill has been repeatedly repudiated by later ornithologists.]

"The Chuck-will's-widow manifests a strong antipathy towards all snakes, however harmless they may be. Although these birds cannot in any way injure the snakes, they alight near them and try to frighten them away, by opening their prodigious mouths and emitting a strong hissing murmur. It was after witnessing one of these occurrences at early twilight that the idea of painting these birds in such a situation struck me. The beautiful little snake, gliding along the dead branch between two birds, a male and a female, is commonly called the *Harlequin Snake* [coral snake]."

Audubon's keen observation is scarcely anywhere more evident than in this paragraph at the close of his essay on the whippoorwill, melodious cousin of the chuck-will's-widow:

"It is a remarkable fact that even the largest moths on which the Whip-poor-will feeds are always swallowed tail foremost, and afterward the wings and legs are found closely laid together, as if partially glued by the gastric juice of the bird. The act of deglutition must be greatly aided by the long bristly feathers of the upper mandible, as these no doubt force the wings of the insects close together, before they enter the mouth. In the *Birds of America* I have represented a male and two females, as well as some of the insects on which they feed. The former are placed on a branch of red oak, a tree abundant on the skirts of the Kentucky Barrens, where the Whip-poor-will is most plentiful."

Audubon skillfully described the flight of every bird. These recitals virtually re-create aerial motion, as well as the bird's instinctive pursuit of prey. Such details are as fully treated as coloration and other physical characters consonant with intimate knowledge. Of interest in connection with insects is his vignette of the feeding ritual of the American redstart:

"This is one of the most lively and handsome of our fly-catchers. It ornaments our woods over the whole of the United States [of the time of writing]. It keeps in perpetual motion, hunting along the branches sidewise, jumping to either side in search of insects and larvae, opening its beautiful tail at every movement which it makes, then closing it, and flirting it from side to side, just allowing the transparent beauty of the feathers to be seen for a moment. The wings now gently droop and the sounds, 'tetee-whee, tetee-whee,' are emitted. Should it see an insect on the wing, it immediately flies in pursuit of it, mounting in the air or coming towards the ground spirally and in many zig-zags. The insect secured, the lovely Redstart reascends, perches, and sings a different note, equally clear, 'wizz, wizz, wizz.' While following insects on the wing, it keeps its bill constantly open, snapping as if it caught several on the same excursion. It frequently balances in the air, opposite a bunch of leaves, and darts into the midst of them after the insects concealed there."

Audubon's portrait of the redstart is memorable for the exquisite detail of paper wasps and their nest, shown on page 66. The inclusion of the nest warranted this comment from the painter: "I have looked for several minutes at a time on the ineffectual attacks which this bird makes on wasps while busily occupied about their own nests. The bird approaches and snaps at them, but in vain; for the wasp, while elevating its abdomen, protrudes its sting, which prevents its being seized. The male bird is represented in the plate in this picture."

Often the descriptions afford clear impressions of surrounding country. "The Blue-grey Fly-catcher [today called the blue-gray gnat-catcher] arrives in the neighborhood of New Orleans about the middle of March, when it is seen along the water courses, flitting about and searching diligently amidst the branches of the golden willow for the smaller kinds of winged insects, devouring great numbers of mosquitoes among others. . . . This diminutive, lively bird is frequently the nurse or foster parent of the young Cow Bunting, whose real mother drops her egg in its nest. . . . It seldom visits the interior of our forests, but prefers the skirts of woods along damp or swampy places and the borders of creeks, pools or rivers. It seizes insects on the wing with great ability, making little sallies after those tiny flies which seem as if dancing in the air, and which cross one another in their lines of flight in a thousand various ways. . . . In the plate I have represented a twig of one of our most valuable trees and its pendulous blossoms, the black walnut. The wood is used for furniture, and the stocks of muskets are generally made of it. The fruit, in a very hard shell, is thought good by many people."

The spider is no longer regarded as an insect but occupies a zoological division of its own. In Audubon's day, however, no such distinction was made. For him, the spider's interest lay in its relation to the life history of American birds, where, sometimes, it is victor rather than vanquished.

Not long ago, in Audubon's old Kentucky hunting country, the writer heard a tale of a spider which may have had its counterpart in the naturalist's observations. A farmer on the edge of the blue grass, seeing a bird-catching spider throw a web around a hummingbird, rushed to the bird's rescue, breaking the web. The spider quickly shuffled off as the brilliant little nectar-feeder flew free for a short distance, then of a sudden turned back to touch the farmer's hand.

Audubon's journal of his river journey of 1821 offers this note on an incident witnessed near New Orleans: "We saw a singularly rich colored spider that, finding a horse-fly just entangled in her net, move to it and cover it in a moment with the silk of her bag, shooting it out in a stream and at the same time rolling the fly until the whole resembled a small oblong of white silk. The spider then returned to the center of its net. No doubt this is a way of preserving the flies when the spider is not hungry." All who know the *Birds of America* are well acquainted with those birds intently watching spiders on their webs. Here, to accompany them, are passages to show how Audubon wrote of these creatures which figure impressively in his sketchbook:

"On a fine evening nearly at sunset, at the end of August, on the banks of the Delaware in New Jersey below Camden, I found the pair of Connecticut Warblers which appear in the plate for the *Birds*. They were hopping and skipping from one low bush to another among the tall reeds of the marsh, emitting an often-repeated 'tweet' at every move. They were chasing a species of spider which runs nimbly over the water, and which they caught by gliding over it, as a Swallow does when drinking. I followed them for about a hundred yards. I outlined both of them by candle-light that evening, and finished the drawing next morning by breakfast time. On opening them I counted upwards of fifty of the spiders mentioned above, but not any other food. This pair had seemed to take very little notice of me, although at times I had been quite close. The plant on which they are placed in the picture, the wild gentian, grew abundantly on the spot where I procured them."

Audubon repeatedly revealed his awareness of aquatic insects as a separate division. He refers to them as such in his fine essay for his plate of the "Carolina Wren." Hard indeed it is to realize that this tiny being dares to become the regular and successful challenger of lizards in addition to insects and spiders. Audubon's partiality to it for this and certain other rather more endearing characteristics is clearly attested to where he writes of it as a traveling companion:

"The quick motion of this active little bird is fully equal to that of the mouse. Like the latter, it appears and is out of sight in a moment, peeps into a crevice, passes rapidly through it, and shows itself at a different place the next instant. When satiated, or fatigued by its multiplied exertions, the little fellow stops, drops its tail and sings a short ditty resembling 'come-to-me, come-to-me,' several times in quick succession, so loud and yet so mellow that it is always agreeable to listen. During spring these notes are heard from all parts of the plantations, the damp woods, the swamps, the

sides of creeks and rivers, as well as from the barns, stables and piles of wood within a few yards of the house.

"I frequently heard these Wrens singing from the roof of an abandoned flat-boat, fastened to the shore a small distance below New Orleans. When its song was finished, the bird went on creeping from one board to another, thrust itself through an auger-hole, entered through the boat's side at one place, and peeped out at another, catching numerous spiders and insects all the while. It sometimes ascends to the higher branches of a tree by climbing along a grapevine, searching diligently amongst the leaves and in the chinks of the bark, alighting sidewise against the trunk and moving like a true Creeper.... Amongst the many species of insects which they destroy, several are of an aquatic nature, found in masses of drift wood. . . . Whilst at 'Oakley,' the residence of my friend James Pirrie, Esq., near Bayou Sarah, I discovered one of these Wrens roosting in a Wood Thrush's nest on a low horizontal branch. The nest had been filled with leaves that had fallen during the autumn. The Wren was in the habit of thrusting his body beneath the leaves, and I doubt not found the place very comfortable."

In the prose which mirrors the captivating "House Wren" and its insect quests, one may catch an intimate glimpse of young John James and his wife at her home, Fatland Ford, in Pennsylvania:

"The familiarity of the House Wren is extremely pleasing. In Pennsylvania a pair of these birds had formed a nest, and the female was sitting in a hole of the wall within a few inches of my (literally so-called) drawing-room. The male was continually singing within a few feet of my wife and myself, whilst I was engaged in portraying birds of other species. When the window was open, its company was extremely agreeable, as was its little song which continually reminded us of its happy life. It would now and then dive into the garden at the foot of the window, for food for its mate, return and creep into the hole where it had its nest, and be off again in a moment. I sometimes threw some flies and spiders towards him. He would eat some himself with great alacrity and carry the rest to his mate. He became more acquainted with us daily, entered the room, and once or twice sang whilst there. One morning I took him in to draw his portrait, and after suddenly closing the window, I easily caught him in my hand and finished his likeness, after which I restored him to liberty." (Audubon's ambidextrous command made this quite easy.) "This, however, made him more cautious, and he never again ventured within the window, although he sang and looked at us as at first."

Audubon also had a proper regard for the brilliant hummingbirds, though they were not his absolute favorites. Blessed with more surface beauty than most of the winged tribe, this dazzling charmer has not, it must be conceded, the wild grandeur of flight or lovely song of some of its fellows. His tribute, voiced as if by a connoisseur or jeweler rather than a wind-swept poet, is highly engaging, a vivid delineation in words of this insect-like bird:

"Where is the person who, on seeing this lovely little creature moving on humming winglets through the air, suspended as if by magic in it, flitting from one flower to another—where is the person, I ask you, who on observing this glittering fragment of the rainbow would not instantly turn his mind with reverence toward the Almighty Creator? Everywhere we observe his sublime conceptions and manifestations in his admirable system of creation.

"No sooner has the returning sun again introduced the vernal season and caused millions of plants to expand their leaves and blossoms than the little Humming-bird is seen advancing on fairy wings. It visits every opening flower-cup, removing from each the injurious insects that otherwise would ere long cause their beauteous petals to droop and decay. Poised in the air, it peeps cautiously and with sparkling eye into their innermost recesses, the ethereal motions of its pinions, so rapid and so light, appearing to fan and cool the flower without injuring its fragile texture. The delightful murmuring sound is well adapted for lulling the insects to repose. Then is the moment for the Humming-bird to secure them. Its long delicate bill enters the cup of the flower, and the protruding double-tubed, delicately sensible tongue, imbued with a glutinous saliva, touches each insect in succession, and draws it out. All this is done in a moment, and as the bird leaves the flower it sips so small a portion of its liquid honey that the theft, we may suppose, is looked upon gratefully by the flower, kindly relieved of destroyers. . . .

"The gorgeous throat of the little bird glows with a fiery hue, and then changes to the deepest velvety black. The upper parts of its delicate body are of resplendent changing green. It throws itself through the air with a swiftness and vivacity hardly conceivable. It moves from one flower to another like a gleam of light. I wish it were in my power to impart to you the pleasure I have felt while watching a pair engaged in demonstrating their love to each other, the male swelling his plumage and throat and dancing on the wing around the delicate female. He transfers to her bill the insect and the honey with which he seeks to please her. He dares to give chase to the Tyrant Fly-catcher, drives the Blue-bird and the Martin into their boxes, and then he joyously returns on humming pinions to the side of his lovely mate.

"I have seen a newly hatched pair of young, little larger than humble-bees, naked, blind, and so feeble they could scarcely raise their little bill to receive food from the parents. . . .

"A person standing in a garden will be surprised to hear the humming of their wings, then see the birds a few feet from him, and he will be astonished by the rapidity with which they rise into the air and out of sight. They do not alight on the ground, but settle on twigs and branches and move sidewise in prettily measured steps, opening and closing their wings frequently, pluming, shaking and arranging their apparel with neatness and activity. They are particularly fond of spreading one wing at a time, and of passing each quill-feather through their bill its whole length, and if the sun is shining the wing is rendered extremely transparent and light. They leave the twig in an instant, and as if with superior powers of vision they make directly for a Martin or Blue-bird fifty or sixty yards away before these birds are even aware of their approach. No bird seems to resist their attacks, but they are sometimes chased by the larger humble-bees, of which they seldom take the least notice. Their superiority of flight enables them to leave these slow moving insects far behind in the short space of a minute. . . .

"Their food consists principally of insects, generally of the coleopterous or beetle order, and diminutive flies, the former in flowers, the latter on the wing. The nectar or honey of the flowers, being not enough to support them, is used more as if to allay their thirst. I have seen many of these birds kept in partial confinement . . . and supplied twice a day with fresh flowers in a room with windows covered with netting through which minute insects could enter. After twelve months the person in lower Louisiana who kept them gave them their liberty. . . .

"The Humming-bird does not shun mankind so much as birds generally do. It frequently approaches flowers in windows, or even in rooms when the windows are open, during the extreme heat of the day, and it returns when not interrupted, as long as the flowers are unfaded. They are extremely abundant in Louisiana during spring and summer, and wherever a fine trumpet-flower is found in the woods, one or more are generally to be seen about it, and now and then as many as ten or twelve. The quarrelsome males have frequent battles in the air. Should one be feeding on a flower and another approach, they both immediately rise in the air, twittering and twirling in a spiral until out of sight. The conflict over, the victor immediately returns to the flower.

"If you would form an idea of their peculiar mode of flight and of their appearance when on the wing, I would say that the large sphinx moth, were it the same color as these birds, comes nearer to the Humming-bird, when moving from flower to flower, than anything I know. . . . I have represented several of these pretty and most interesting birds feeding, caressing each other, or sitting on the slender stalks of the trumpet-flower and pluming themselves. The diversity of action and attitude may, I trust, prove sufficient to present a faithful idea of their appearance and manners."

Insect and Incident

Philadelphia, when Audubon arrived there in April, 1824, in search of support for his publishing plans, was America's pioneer center of science. Although Say was then a resident of the city, it is interesting that it should have been Titian Peale's name which creeps more often into Audubon's journal during the latter's six-month visit. Say, at the time, was publishing *American Entomology*, and many of Peale's drawings were included.

Audubon went first to the home of a friend of his youth, Dr. William Mease, who introduced him to the twenty-one-year-old ornithologist of promise, Charles Lucien Bonaparte, to whom reference has already been made. The Prince of Musignano, as Bonaparte was also known, expressed intense admiration for Audubon's drawings and took him to a meeting of the Academy of Natural Sciences so that he might have the opportunity of impressing its members with his work. The assembled company, however, viewed the pictures with mixed enthusiasm. Titian Peale, who had seen Audubon's pre-Feliciana drawings in Cincinnati, and who was now primarily engaged in illustrating Bonaparte's *American Ornithology,* not only felt jealousy at his employer's interest in a rival undertaking, but, being a follower of the Wilson tradition of straight bird profiles minus any dramatic posing, considered himself the superior artist. His brother, Rembrandt Peale, liked the drawings notwithstanding.

George Ord, leader of the worshipful and self-interested Wilson publishing coterie, was openly hostile at the presentation. Brooking no rivals of Alexander Wilson, the Scottish-born ornithologist, a new edition of whose works Ord was hoping shortly to issue, he pronounced Audubon's compositions combining insects, branches, and flowers with attitudinizing birds a distortion of Wilson's ideal method of unadorned profiles. Alexander Lawson, Ord's engraver, followed suit, refusing to have anything to do with the intruder's plans and calling his drawing anatomically incorrect, "too soft," and too much like oil painting in effect.

Another engraver, however, named Fairman, demonstrated his sympathetic attitude by hiring Audubon to draw a small grouse for the decoration of a New Jersey bank-note engraving. This had very fortunate consequences. Edward Harris, a prosperous gentleman farmer of nearby Moorestown, New Jersey, upon seeing the new bank note, sought Audubon out, and a lifelong friendship resulted. Not only did Harris help the artist financially, but he joined him on two future expeditions. Meanwhile Fairman urged Audubon to try to reach Europe, that he might find an engraver able to meet the admittedly difficult requirements that his dramatic technique imposed.

To return once more to Titian Peale, it should be remarked that Audubon's opinion of his bird pictures was one of reciprocal distaste, which he wisely confided only to his journal. The rivals managed, at least socially, to disguise their undoubted professional rivalry. When Peale politely refused to show Audubon a certain rare bird in his collection, Audubon wrote: "This little incident filled me with grief at the narrow spirit of humanity and makes me wish for the solitude of the woods." But the refusal apparently left him undaunted. From the point of view of posterity, he had nothing to fear from Peale and knew it well. Upon his return to the United States from Great Britain in 1829, it is recorded that he and Peale went birding together on the Jersey coast. In 1836, another entry states that Peale had given him a "new Rallus and six young ones and plenty more."

When the *Birds* were all but finished and he had found time to write a paper on the geographical distribution of North American species, Audubon did not hesitate to call on Peale for assistance, asking for his list of all the Pennsylvania birds. Even in the 1840's we hear him appealing to his friend for a drawing of a deer species for the *Quadrupeds,* though there is no evidence that he ever obtained it.

Charles Alexandre Lesueur, already introduced, who designed the romantic cover for Say's book and drew some of its best illustrations, was one of those who admired Audubon's portfolio from the start. Like others, he urged Audubon to go to Europe, promising him a note of introduction to the great flower painter, Pierre Joseph Redouté of Paris. This promise he kept on Audubon's departure for England in 1826.

Lesueur, an example of whose artistry may be seen on page 86, made the first study of Great Lakes fishes and was an established scientist before he came to the Philadelphia Academy of Natural Sciences from a West Indies expedition. When the Academy's president, Maclure, boarded the keelboat which carried a load of learned followers of the visionary Owen to his socialist colony in New Harmony, Indiana, in 1825, Lesueur as well as Say and Peale sailed with him. While there, Lesueur worked on Say's illustrations; and, when the colony dissolved after two turbulent years, he stayed on with Say who became the defunct colony's property agent. He made an intensive study of the mound builder remains of the region, while willingly sharing the eccentrically frugal existence of Say and his wife. Some of his delicate water-color sketches of local scenes may still be seen in New Harmony. His design for the theater drop of the Thespian Society, showing Niagara, a rainbow, lightning, and a rattlesnake, was repeated on tickets for the first performance. Soon after the death of Say in Indiana in 1834, Lesueur returned to France. But he and Audubon continued to keep in touch.

While Audubon was in Philadelphia his "dear friend" and assistant of Mississippi expedition days, young Joseph Mason, called to see him. On this occasion Mason, by then seventeen, and painting flowers for Barton's Gardens, fell to reminiscing with the naturalist, and looked at many of the drawings on which the two had worked together. Upon seeing Audubon's name in ink on some, and his own either in pencil or erased on certain others, Mason's pride was so hurt that he declined an invitation to go South with him again. Feeling increasingly bitter over this slight, he began to talk of it freely, letting Ord and Audubon's other enemies know. The rumor of the extent of the boy's assistance shortly became public knowledge, and soon it swelled beyond reason. That Mason was responsible for many flowers for which he received no credit cannot be denied. But it has never been suggested that Audubon, having taught Mason much of what he knew about art, may have redrawn and reworked some of the flower details until he felt he had made them his own.

Because of his failure to obtain backing for the publication of his drawings, it was a disconsolate Audubon who left Philadelphia in August, 1824. But the months of effort had been more fruitful than he realized. He had made a number of enduring friendships. The one with Edward Harris, who put cash in his hands at a moment of acute need, and to whom he showed his gratitude by presenting him with all his early drawings of

French birds, was to come forward again and again with encouragement and funds. Lesueur, Bonaparte, Harlan, and even Titian Peale in his fashion, had befriended him and continued to be valuable connections. The noted Thomas Sully had also given him free lessons in the use of oils, inadvertently furthering the cause of the *Birds* by providing a new and much needed means of revenue.

One cannot help wondering whether Ord's disparaging remarks about the inclusion of insects in the drawings for the *Birds* made it easier for Audubon to part with his sketchbook in Pittsburgh so soon after leaving Philadelphia. Another possibility presents itself. Audubon's aspirations were usually all-inclusive—to portray *all* the birds, all the quadrupeds. Had he entertained any such idea as to insects and reptiles (and this is doubtful), he must have learned from Say that American insect species were too multitudinous and far spread for full treatment by that pioneering generation. Also, he had completed most of the Lower Mississippi birds with their insect details and could spare this handsome "bread and butter" token. But later on, in the 1830's at the home of the Bachmans in Charleston, where insects were of considerable interest, he may have regretted that the album was no longer his.

In New York, where he went directly from Pittsburgh, no publisher would so much as consent to look at his drawings. After a few fruitless and unpromising days, he took a Hudson River boat up to Albany with the idea of trying to interest Governor De Witt Clinton in his birds. But that, too, proved futile. The nature-loving official was out of the city. The artist thereupon decided to continue northward to see Niagara, and carry out his ambition to paint the Falls. But the wonder of the spectacle discouraged him from trying. No painter, he averred, could imitate its grandeur. From Buffalo he went by boat to Erie, sleeping on deck in his buffalo robe, lacking the price of a cabin and too proud to accept the captain's kind offer of shelter for which he could not pay. On reaching Erie he soon set out for Pittsburgh, his spirits elevated by the company of an itinerant artist met along the way. After surrendering five of his precious dollars to a carter to carry himself and friend and their belongings to Meadville, Audubon was so reduced that the carter offered the two artists the shelter of his home in that village. By keeping their crayons busy, the two artists soon increased the mere twenty cents between them to a sum sufficient to permit them to set out on foot for Pittsburgh, reached after two days of walking. The time of year was early September. Mrs. Basham came to the rescue, as we have seen, and her own and her daughter's reward was the gift of the sketchbook.

Constantine Rafinesque, "Odd Fish"

Insects occasionally fly into the pages of Audubon's journals and letters, both in his Henderson, Kentucky, days and years later in the British Isles. At the time of an unexpected visit to him in Henderson from Constantine Rafinesque, "odd fish," botanist, and student of fishes, an extraordinary beetle figured in the episode.

"It was summer," wrote Audubon, "and the windows were all open. The light of the candles attracted many insects, among which was a large kind of beetle. I caught one, and aware of Rafinesque's inclination to believe only what he himself should see, I showed him the insect, assuring him that it was so strong that it would crawl on the table with a candlestick on its back. 'I should like to see this done, Mr. Audubon,' my guest replied. The experiment was made, and the insect moved about, dragging its burden in such a way that the candle seemed to be moving as if by magic, until, coming to the table's edge, the beetle dropped on the floor, took to wing, and escaped." That night in Rafinesque's bedroom, insects and a bat were attracted by the light, whereupon the "Daniel Boone of science," ever on the lookout for something new, took Audubon's precious Cremona to the velvet-winged mammal, dashing the violin to pieces.

Audubon is often severely criticized for his practical joke on Rafinesque. He gave him drawings of ten nonexistent fish to copy in his notebook. These baffled and confused scientists for fully half a century. But was the ruined Cremona not provocation enough for such a prank? The answer depends on one's preferences. Whatever these may be, there can be no doubt that music played second fiddle to bats in the minds of Audubon's critics.

John George Children, English Friend

Not long after his arrival in England in 1826, Audubon's encounter with a butterfly at York nearly cost him his "American stick," a cane with a sword inside it. "During my early walk along the Ouse River," he wrote, "I saw a large butterfly, quite new to me, and attempted to procure it with a stroke of my cane. But as I whirled it round, off went the scabbard into the river, more than half across, and I stood with a naked sword as if waiting for a duel. I would have swam out for it, but that there were other pedestrians; so a man in a boat brought it to me for sixpence."

Audubon, while abroad, was a kind of free agent for his friends wanting specimens of every kind. He would write to his sons and ask for shells for his engraver's use in connection with the *Birds*. Havell, in the course of his work, found a demand for shells on the London market, a discovery which caused Audubon to write for more—"thousands" more. Once, after visiting the United States, he brought a live alligator, intended as a gift, aboard the *Texas*, but it expired on reaching Liverpool. The ten live turtles that he kept in his "little back yard" were also to be presents. No less spectacular was the shipping of 1,150 trees to England, fourteen live opossums, and a wild turkey. That he brought birds with varying success and in wide variety goes without saying.

No friend in England proved more helpful professionally than insect-collecting John George Children of the British Museum. When he and the painter met, Children was secretary of the Royal Society, to which he introduced Audubon and the first of the engravings for the *Birds*. Audubon sold him a rare proof set of the First Number of ten plates which were engraved by Lizars of Edinburgh, untouched by Havell, who would presently "edit" Lizars' initial efforts. Children paid two guineas for the number—Audubon's first sale after years of labor. Not only was he instrumental in making Audubon a Royal Society member, but he saw to it that the king took notice of the "woodsman's" vast undertaking.

In Leeds the painter wrote on September 30, 1827: "The King! My dear Book! It was presented to him by Sir Walter Waller, Bart., K.C.H., at the request of my most excellent friend J. G. Children. His Majesty was pleased to call it fine, permitted me to publish it under his particular patronage, approbation, and protection, became a subscriber on the usual terms, not as kings usually do, but as a gentleman."

Then in 1829 when Audubon found a return trip to America essential to obtain more birds, Children consented to look after his interests in London as to engravings and subscriptions. The mild, genial Children had been his confidant when press attacks were being made on him in England and Philadelphia for certain addresses and papers. He had persuaded Audubon to ignore abusive and polemical letters, and to stick to the writing of his bird biographies as a worthier outlet for his energy. Children had also tactfully convinced the long-haired and picturesque "American woodsman"—as Audubon delighted to be known—that he must quit carrying his huge portfolio of drawings on his shoulder in "proper" London. He had been accustomed to doing this unashamedly in New York and, as he wrote, "even tenacious Philadelphia." Children said that he must hire a cab or porter, if for his dignity alone.

From the spring of 1829 until 1834, Audubon's letters alluded often to shipments of boxes of insects by the thousands for Children. He was frequently writing—to his sons or to Dr. Harlan—or else bringing insects himself from his visits to the United States. His close association with Children must inevitably have extended his knowledge of entomology. While he was in New York in 1833 his thoughts were not only on obtaining more boxes of insects for his friend, among other missions, but on certain insects for his *Birds*. "You must stick a Cricket or a Grasshopper on a thorn before the bill of the male Shrike on the wing," [2] he wrote his son Victor who was then in London supervising the engravings. "It is their habit—but I could not procure one yesterday, and today it rains hard."

Maria Martin, Painter

Influential though Children proved, the zoologist played a far less telling part in forwarding the *Birds of America* than another personality almost completely unknown to the public. That individual, and a rare personality she was—Maria Martin of Charleston, South Carolina—may well have been the most influential woman on the American nineteenth century natural history horizon. First as the sister-in-law of the Reverend John Bachman, who helped write the text of the *Quadrupeds,* then later on in

2 Plate XCII of a shrike shows a grasshopper in *The Birds of America.*

1849 as his wife, Miss Martin more than deserves the recognition so long denied her.

Audubon's chance meeting with Bachman in October, 1831, led to the clergyman's taking him and his two assistants into his home for several weeks when they were financially embarrassed. Apparently Maria was already interested in painting, but beginning in December of that same year, when he wrote that she was drawing a bird, her name began to crop up regularly in Audubon's letters, indicating continuous activity. While Bachman, an ardent naturalist who eventually won himself a reputation on two continents by his erudite writings on science subjects, was helping Audubon with ornithological problems, Maria Martin drew flowers, branches, and some insects for use in the engravings.

Maria, a permanent guest in the large Bachman mansion, soon entered into regular correspondence with Lucy Audubon, becoming a close friend of the entire family. Later the tie was strengthened even more when Audubon's sons married the two eldest Bachman daughters. Audubon, who often wrote Maria while in England, kept her supplied with suitable brushes and art materials, as well as with plentiful hints as to how they should be employed. Examples of her skill, reproduced in this book, suggest why he happened to write of her as he did to Victor in 1833 from Charleston. "Miss Martin, with her superior talents, assists us greatly in the way of drawing; the insects she has drawn are, perhaps, the best I've seen." His letters to Bachman spoke of her as "your Sister our Dear Sweetheart," and in them he would plead for more fine floral backgrounds. Her "White Hibiscus," "Red Hibiscus," "Nondescript Rose," "Begonia," and "Sylvia" pleased both Audubon and Bachman.

In the little-known, scarce, and seldom consulted text of the *Birds of America*, Audubon credited Maria Martin with several of the insect and flower accessories, those for the "Brown-headed Worm-eating Warbler," "Bachman's Swamp Warbler," the "Band-tailed Dove," the "Yellow-crowned Night Heron," and the nest for the "Ruffnecked Humming-bird." She also painted the habitat for the "Columbian Humming-bird," page 60. The first named, actually Swainson's warbler, is of additional interest in that the bird should have been credited to John Woodhouse Audubon. No part of the plate is by Audubon senior. Maria Martin received credit for its botany and insects in his *Birds* text; the rest of the story about this plate emerges in a letter from Audubon to his engraver, dated Charleston, November 24, 1833: ". . . John, myself and Miss Martin . . . are drawing constantly, to finish all the unfinished Drawings now on hand; I think that 30 days hence, that task will be accomplished. John draws sufficiently well for publication now, and one Drawing of a New Species, named after Swainson, will be in the 2nd Volume. It will reach you in time for that purpose with two others. . . ."

Audubon buried another salient admission in the text of his *Birds*. All plants and branches for the seventy or so western bird species from the Townsend-Nuttall collection were apparently by Miss Martin. Unless she had lent her assistance in the eleventh hour, the virtually impossible could not have been accomplished by 1838! On account of the pressure of time, some of these habitats had to be little more than bare boughs and branches. When the 350th plate of the great work was finished on copper in June, 1836, Audubon wrote to Bachman: ". . . I much wish your Dear Sister, our Sweetheart, would draw plants and branches of Trees for me to the number of fifteen or twenty drawings for the small plates [the miniature edition of the *Birds*, then planned]. Anything not published in my Two first Volumes would prove a valuable acquisition, and she should send five or six at a time . . . care of Havell. . . . Our Victor would know how to use them by placing them [with] Birds which I have drawn without plants."

Audubon also neglected to credit Maria specifically with the pair of butterflies for "MacGillivray's Seaside Sparrow." Her originals for this detail are reproduced for the first time on page 86. They were painted on one page of a sketchbook which she gave to Audubon, and which may for all we know have contained several other details later incorporated in the *Birds*. The surviving pages are now owned by the Charleston Museum.

On some of these pages, as well as on those of a companion sketchbook, is Maria Martin's longhand transcript of the text of Say's *American Entomology*, with her accompanying water-color copies. Only six out of her fifty-four copies of Say's plates are missing—destroyed with an indeterminate number of other studies in her first sketchbook, which was damaged when Lucy Audubon's cottage burned to the ground in 1875 a year after her passing. In the remaining material, and in the back of the second book (complete and in good condition), we also find random insect drawings— twenty-nine figures in all—obviously made from nature.

Maria's industrious study of Say's illustrations represents an important link to Audubon. She undoubtedly copied them for practice before helping him with some of the insects of the *Birds*. Say's book came out in 1824-1828; Audubon met Bachman late in 1831; Maria's butterflies for the sparrow in Plate CCCLV, mentioned above, were engraved in 1837; therefore her two sketchbooks would seem to date between 1833 and 1836 or thereabouts. Audubon's letter from Baltimore to Bachman in 1836, indicating the clergyman's anxiety to obtain butterflies for his collection, remarks: "I have a few butterflies for you from Nuttall!" Perhaps two of Maria's sketches faintly labeled "Florida" came from that distinguished scientist and explorer, Thomas Nuttall, via Audubon.

Later, in connection with Audubon's *Quadrupeds*, the important part Maria played in helping Bachman edit the text is highlighted in a letter to Audubon: "Maria knocks to the right and left with your articles and mine—lops off, corrects, criticizes, abuses and praises by turn," Bachman wrote. "She does wonders." Later on he called her his "amanuensis," a name he repeated in 1849 when, after being widowed for some years, he was about to marry Maria. An injury to his eyes caused him to "borrow" her vision, that the work might go forward. Maria herself was often ill during that period, yet she would hide Bachman's spectacles to make him rest, while she herself did everything she could to help.

There is little possibility of confusing Mason's flowers with those of

Maria Martin. Mason worked for the *Birds* a decade before Audubon met the Bachmans and Miss Martin, late in 1831. Many of the originals of the Louisiana period, when Mason was with Audubon, are signed and dated. The date on the engraved plates is, naturally, always later than the originals. Stylistically, many flowers of the small edition of the *Birds* can be attributed to Miss Martin, even without the encouragement of the letter from Audubon, already quoted, about his need for such assistance. In the writer's opinion, such flowers of the *Birds of America* as are positively attributable to Audubon prove him not only the peer of his flower-painting helpers—Mason, Lehman, and Miss Martin—but their true master, able though they were.

Many details and accessories which appear in the engravings are not to be seen in the original Audubon drawings at the New York Historical Society. The exquisite caterpillar and flying night moths—added later to the "Whip-poor-will," and illustrated on page 85—were simply indicated by their names at the proper points in the composition, "Io," and "Cecropia." The original, from the early Louisiana period, was painted long before its engraving in 1830. The original for the "White-headed Eagle" (Plate XXXI of the *Birds*) shows the eagle devouring a Canada goose, but in the engraving the goose was replaced with a large catfish. The catfish, in the original of the "Bald Eagle" (Plate CXXVI), disappeared in the engraving and was not replaced with any other creature. In the 1821 original of the "American Egret" (Plate CCCLXXXVI) a crayfish was painted, but it was replaced, when the painting was engraved years later, by a lizard obtained from Dr. Richard Harlan, the "Tapayaxin." Both flowers and insects for Plate XXXII, the "Black-billed Cuckoo," appear in the original and the engraving. These are by Mason, who claimed them long after he helped Audubon on this handsome bird portrait in Louisiana. The paper wasps and their nest, shown with the "Orchard Oriole," was included in both the original sketch and the print. The lilies engraved with the "Whistling Swan" are of interest not only because they are absent in the original but because for years their authenticity was challenged by botanists who, in the end, proved to be mistaken.

Not only did Maria Martin draw details for Audubon, but, for a while, she had the prosaic task of handling his cash and a large group of his drawings. "Kiss our dear Sweetheart for me!" he would write in many a letter to Bachman, and well he might! Nevertheless, there is every reason to suspect that Audubon, Bachman, and Maria herself died without the slightest intimation that she would one day come in for any such recognition as this chapter clearly intends for her. It is doubtful whether any American female acolyte of science accomplished as much in her century. In our own, she has helped popularize ornithology by her charming additions to Audubon's *Birds*. Like the many who shared his enormously ambitious and diversified tasks, her name deserves to live along with his. Entomologists, it is certain, will regard her insect drawings with respect for their painstaking accuracy and skill.

NIGHT-FLYING MOTHS. *Left*: IO, *Automeris io*. *Right*: CECROPIA, *Samia cecropia*. Painted near Natchez in 1822. (Facsimile detail from the "Whip-poor-will" plate in the *Birds* folio.)

Here, and on pages 88 to 92, works of American contemporaries in insect illustration (Lesueur, Wood, Peale) are reproduced for the purpose of comparing the earliest works in the field of American entomology. The art of Maria Martin, who was not only Audubon's contemporary but his assistant in the drawing of insects and bird habitats, also appears.

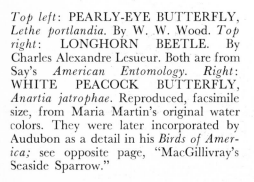

Top left: PEARLY-EYE BUTTERFLY, *Lethe portlandia*. By W. W. Wood. *Top right*: LONGHORN BEETLE. By Charles Alexandre Lesueur. Both are from Say's *American Entomology*. *Right*: WHITE PEACOCK BUTTERFLY, *Anartia jatrophae*. Reproduced, facsimile size, from Maria Martin's original water colors. They were later incorporated by Audubon as a detail in his *Birds of America;* see opposite page, "MacGillivray's Seaside Sparrow."

(Charleston Museum)

BLUE SWALLOWTAIL BUTTERFLY, *Papilio philenor*. By Titian Peale, for Say's *American Entomology*, first American book on insects. Audubon met Say and Peale while at work on his *Birds*.

TIGER SWALLOWTAIL BUTTERFLY, *Papilio glaucus*. By Titian Peale. Say and Peale, pioneering in entomology, paralleled Audubon's early study of our birds in relation to insects.

Above: SWALLOWTAIL BUT-
TERFLY, *Papilio polydamas*. By
Maria Martin. Natural size.

Left: SPHINX MOTH, *Pholus
pandorus*. By Maria Martin. Natural size.

Opposite page: MILLER
MOTH, *Erebus odora*. By Maria
Martin. Natural size.

These water colors by Miss Martin are interesting, coming from
the hand of one of Audubon's
ablest helpers. (See page 81.)

BUTTERFLY, *Junonia coenia*. By Maria Martin for "Swainson's Warbler" in the *Birds* folio. Facsimile detail. No part of the plate is by Audubon; the bird was by his son John.

John Children was not Audubon's only reminder in London of the western world's growing attention to insects. Neither man would live to explore Darwin's theory of the origin of species of 1859, which affected all branches of zoology with regard to evolution. But that the trend was more and more to insects is unmistakable in Audubon's letters to John Bachman. "Insects are now very high," he wrote in 1834. "I paid 20 Dollars the other day for 5 which, on account of their beauty, my friend William Swainson the ornithologist thought cheap." He added that Swainson already owned "upwards of 50,000 Insects and more bird skins than his house will hold." He was shocked to discover that an amateur with a "fine collection of insects" near Leeds had scarcely any knowledge of their *"proper names."*

The following spring he wrote Bachman a letter so entertaining and so humorously philosophical about the contemporary science scene, including some prescient comments on the future, that it is offered herewith almost in full:

"Here there are at present three works being published on the birds of Europe—one by Mr. Gould and the other by no one knows who—at least I do not know. Works on the birds of *all* the World are innumerable—cheap as dirt and more dirty than dirt. Sir William Jardine will encumber the whole of God's Creation with stuff as little like the Creator's formations as the moon is unto cheese, but who cares?—as long as these miscellanies bring forth five shillings per volume to the pocket bag of the one who produces them as a Hen that hatches *duck eggs.* I have no doubt that such a one is as much surprised to see his progenitor go to the market as the Hen is at seeing her webbed brood take to the water. But after all, *Ornithological times* are fast going by. By the time my Work will be done the world will have ceased to think that such beings as birds exist under Heaven's canopy.

"Bugs, fishes and reptiles are, and will be, the go for a time. Then geology will move heavily above as well as through the Earth. Africa will cease to be an unknown land. For aught I know, the North passage into the Pacific will become easier of performance to steamers than the passage of one such vehicle is now to the bar of Charleston. People will dive into the Antipodes. Fishes will swim on Earth. Quadrupeds all will fly, and birds, exchanging their present Natures, will build *churches* and again become the rage of the times! . . .

"This afternoon I attended a public auction of sundries. My friend Thomas McCulloch of Pictou, Nova Scotia, had about 400 well *mounted* birds for sale there. All were disposed of—for how much, do you think? Why, not exceeding $50 . . . McCulloch had refused £500 for this collection while in Nova Scotia! He refused $20 six weeks ago for a Snowy Owl which this afternoon produced just 25¢!!—and all this because the world is all agog—for what? For Bugs the size of Water Melons. There is in fact a Bug now in Havell's engraving shop for which the owner asked—how much? You give up? No less than £50 sterling!—$250 for a Beetle. As large as my fist it is true, but nought but a beetle after all. Thirty guineas have been offered and *refused*. I almost wish I could turn into a *Beetle* myself!

"By the way, my friend Melly of Liverpool is here. He has called twice upon us, and he assured me that more than eight months ago he sent you many hundreds of *Insects,* wrote to you, &c, because I had assured him that you would be delighted to enter into a correspondence with him on Entomology. But not a word has he had from you. His insects were shipped direct from Liverpool to Charleston. Look out, my friend, or you will have some Water(ton) [a bad pun on the name of Charles Waterton, Audubon's severest English critic] *beetle* about your ears. Do write my learned friend, who is, besides, an excellent man, and who has a collection of 13,000 species of Insects *named* and *described*."

If such preoccupations and concerns are those of only a "quasi naturalist," as John James Audubon has been called by one archangel of the scientific circle of angels of our time, then that sphere must be a lonely place indeed. Even when his goal drew him away from America's forests to the cities of the British Isles, he continued to eat, sleep, *live* science—learning, listening, teaching and being taught, without end. What he called the disparagement of his qualifications and the belittlement of his efforts by such archangels of his day was, in fact, "smoke from a dung hill."

Audubon himself was not, however, above jealousy and recrimination toward that class of critics which has nursed new animosity toward his achievement with each succeeding generation. A year before the *Birds* was completed, he probably felt he could afford to poke fun at his pretentious surroundings when he wrote these thoughts to Bachman: ". . . a very learned member of the Scientific Association, whilst at Liverpool, and during the learned gathering of that brilliant congregation, discovered a New Plant growing on the very back of a Dead Fly. The Plant being abundant in both hemispheres during winter, I would advise you to muster up a pair of specks and identify the European and American house-fly plant."

Ahead, in his partly disillusioning attempts to expertize upon reptiles, lies reason enough for such acerbity as this.

IV

OF REPTILES

Early Gleanings

IN NORTH AMERICA the science of herpetology, the study of reptiles, had advanced even less than the science of entomology at the time Audubon drew the jewel-like lizards and snake in his sketchbook.

Audubon's observations were quite as acute respecting certain of the reptiles as they were on the insects. On at least two of our common snakes he wrote at length as an eye-witness observer. These creatures he drew also with equal realism and beauty—when they were beautiful—and with horrific truth when horror was demanded. The snake in the sketchbook resembles, in its refinement, some ancient Egyptian necklace of a Cleopatra or Nefertiti. Deceptively small in appearance, its actual length is eighteen inches.

Almost from the year of his arrival in England in 1826, Audubon was to be accused of writing romances or legends about wild life. Yet he was not so much more in the dark as to reptiles than most pretenders to knowledge, especially those notables who attacked him.

The small striped coral snake, shown in a tree with the exceptionally well executed chuck-will's-widow of the *Birds of America,* was called a harlequin by Audubon. Because of the fact that he declared it "quite harmless" it has been suggested that in this instance he perhaps sketched a "mimic" rather than a true coral. This garishly beautiful species is venomous and deadly. The tortuous garter snake writhing in the beak of a soaring swallow-tailed kite in the seventy-second plate of the *Birds,* already remarked upon, inspires mixed awe and admiration. Had the painter elected, instead, to show a timber rattler in the talons of an eagle, he could hardly have done so with more sublimity. His blacksnake worrying a nest of brown thrashers, also in the *Birds,* is entirely in order both as to activity and location, being a climber.

Turning to early American reptilian research, one comes upon the name of John Edwards Holbrook (1794-1871). A graduate in medicine at the University of Pennsylvania, Holbrook went abroad for advanced study, first to the British Isles, then the Continent.

In Paris he fraternized with eminent naturalists who were continuing the outstanding research begun in the previous century by their predecessor Lacépède. The Museum of Natural History and the Jardin des Plantes were the centers of all such activity, led by Baron Cuvier, founder of the study of comparative anatomy. Holbrook's particular friends were

Valenciennes, Bibron and Duméril, though the latter two had yet to write their classic, *General Herpetology, or Complete Natural History of Reptiles,* a nine-volume work begun in 1834 and completed in 1854. They, Blainville, Latreille, Oppel, and others were laboring mightily in France toward a more precise arrangement of the reptilian, serpent, and amphibian groups. The first book on reptiles, one by Laurenti published in Vienna in 1768, was not, after all, so many years behind them.

Holbrook had always inclined toward natural history as an avocation. His brilliant French cronies so stimulated his interest that he began to specialize in reptiles and fishes. All this occurred some years before he met Bachman and Audubon in Charleston, South Carolina, and in fact before Audubon had met Bachman. The latter and also Maria Martin figured in Holbrook's work, too, if far less tellingly than in Audubon's. The doctor of medicine was responsible for the first general work on American reptiles.

We might digress to advantage, here, and take appropriate note of that illustrious acquaintance of both Holbrook and Audubon, none other than Georges Léopold Chrétien Frédéric Dagobert Cuvier, the French baron (1769-1832). It is unlikely that Holbrook's journal, if indeed he kept one, could match Audubon's accounts of his repeated visits at a later date with this famous statesman, author, philosopher, and scientist. Accompanied by the English ornithologist William Swainson and his wife, and also by the painter C. R. Parker, whom he had known in Natchez, Audubon left England late in the summer of 1828 to see subscribers for his *Birds* in Paris.

"We went to the Jardin des Plantes which fronts on a very bad bridge built in the days of Napoleon," his journal relates. "I thought the gardens well laid out, large, handsome, but not everywhere well kept. We saw everything, then walked to the entrance of the famous Musée. It was closed, but we knocked and asked for Baron Cuvier. We were told he was in but too busy to be seen. Being determined to look at the Great Man, we waited, knocked again, and with a certain degree of *firmness* sent our names. The messenger returned, bowed, and led the way upstairs, and in a minute Monsieur le Baron came to us. He had heard much of my friend Swainson and greeted him as he deserves to be greeted. He was polite and kind to me, though my name had never made its way to his ears."

Audubon continued with a verbal sketch of Cuvier which proves him as acute an observer of men as of birds and mammals, concluding: "Thus have I described Cuvier almost as if a *new species* of man." A few days later he and the Swainsons were given tickets to the Museum by the Baron, "and promised all we could wish." Valenciennes was "equally kind," and the naturalist Saint-Hilaire assured him that his bird studies were the "most satisfactory so far," despite the assurance that his name was quite unknown in French scientific circles.

Cuvier introduced Audubon to his family and some fellow Linnaeans at a formal dinner: "There was not the show of opulence that is seen in the same rank of life in England—no, not by far—but it was a good dinner, served *à la française,* with more simplicity than in London. The dinner finished, the Baroness rose and we all followed her into the library. I liked

WHIP-TAIL LIZARD, also known as RACE-RUNNER, *Cnemidophorus*. Western U.S.A. *Left*, dorsal; *right*, ventral. Also head of unidentified reptile from Audubon's sketchbook.

TEEID LIZARD (of *Cnemidophorus* type), native to Central and South America.

opposite page: SNAKE. One of the annulated snakes such as *Leptoderia,* native to Texas, Mexico, Central and South America.

BUFO TOAD.

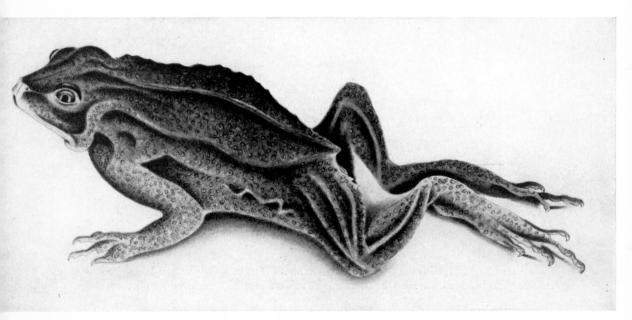

(Photo: Cooper Union Museum)

Top: BROWN SKINK, *Leiolopisma laterale. Center*: GECKO, *Hemidactylus*. Immature specimen. Both from Audubon's sketchbook.

Right: MOCKINGBIRDS and RATTLESNAKE from the *Birds* folio. The inclusion of the rattlesnake in the plate made this one of Audubon's most controversial works (see page 104). The snake was painted at Oakley in 1821 and the picture finished at Beech Woods in 1825.

this much; I cannot bear the *drinking matches* of wine at the English tables. . . . We talked ornithology. He asked me the price of my work."

A day or two later Cuvier saw the *Birds* for the first time: "Baron Cuvier ordered a porter to put my book on a table, and gave me a seat of honor at the Académie Royale des Sciences. The seance opened with a tedious lecture on the vision of the mole. Then Cuvier announced Swainson and me and spoke of my work. It was shown and admired as usual, and Cuvier requested to review it for the 'Mémoires of the Academy.' Poor Audubon! here thou art, a simple woodsman, among a crowd of talented men, yet kindly received by all—so are the works of God as shown in His birds loved by them. I left my book, that the librarian might show it to all who wished to see it. . . . Now, my Lucy, I have certainly run the gauntlet of England and Paris, and may feel proud of two things, that I am considered the first ornithological painter, and the first practical naturalist of America. May God grant me life to accomplish my serious and gigantic work." Not for another ten years would this prayer be answered.

Audubon's admiration is further attested to by the fact that he bought an engraved portrait of Cuvier one day near the Pont des Arts. He also chose a French agent for his project on Cuvier's recommendation, probably after he wrote in his journal: "My work has been seen by many. Cuvier pronounced it the finest of its kind in existence." Considering the activity of Levaillant and others, this was no mean compliment from a man of Cuvier's exalted standing. Audubon had no illusions about the importance of his favor, and he could not be too particular, as the lengthy passages indicate, about setting down the fullest account for his wife's delectation. "I will describe Cuvier's house to thee, Lucy. In the first upstairs room we caught a glimpse of a slight figure dressed all in black, that glided across the floor like a sylph. It was Mademoiselle Cuvier, not quite ready to see the gentlemen: off she flew like a Dove before Falcons. Eight rooms we passed filled with books, each room with a recessed bed. At last we reached a sort of laboratory, the *sanctum sanctorum* of Cuvier. There was nothing in it but books and skeletons of animals, reptiles, etc. His books were in great disorder, as if he read and studied them and owned them for other purposes than show. . . . Cuvier was looking at a small lizard in a tiny vial filled with spirits, his sparkling eye half closed as if quizzing its qualities; he wrote its name on a label, and went on quizzing lizards. . . ."

Two days later he concluded: ". . . I discovered that the Baron thinks himself a fine-looking man. His daughter seemed to know this, and remarked more than once that her father's under lip was swelled more than usual, and she added that the line of his nose was extremely fine. I passed my fingers over mine, and lo! I thought just the same. I see the Baron now, an old green cover-all about him, a neck-cloth that might well surround his body if unfolded, loosely tied about his chin, and his silver locks like those of a man more bent on studying books than on visiting barbers. His fine eyes shot fire from under his bushy eyebrows. . . . I advised Parker who had come to paint Cuvier's portrait, while Mlle. Cuvier read to us, not to keep him long. We adjourned till Sunday. In Connecticut this would be thought horrible, in England difficult, and in Paris the best day for such things."

Holbrook, after settling in Charleston in 1822, helped to found the Medical College of South Carolina, where he served for more than thirty years as an anatomy professor. Though a practicing physician, he never once assisted at or attended a birth, so much did he dislike to see pain. Quite naturally, however, he found it essential in his work to dissect innumerable fishes and reptiles. This man who was to write our first monograph on reptiles was deeply religious, and his lectures on anatomy were said to be more like sermons, stressing the wonder of God's creations—especially the brain. When he set about writing a five-volume work, *Herpetology of the United States,* no previous attempt had been made to cover our species. The only general reference he could consult, a sort of summary by Audubon's old friend Dr. Richard Harlan of Philadelphia, brought out under the aegis of the Academy of that city in 1826-1827, was one so full of pitfalls that it spurred Holbrook onward while helping him very little.

Reptiles of the middle and eastern states and South Carolina had, it is true, been described, but neither the papers nor the figures drawn for them were in accessible publications. Linnaeus, who had listed about thirty species from North America, was among those earlier European zoologists who had worked effectively but by no means exhaustively on the subject. Thomas Say had contributed a little. In 1829 Major LeConte wrote about turtles, touching on about sixty species. But all this effort was sporadic. It remained for Holbrook to unify and extend these efforts. He offered twenty-nine reptiles as new, most of which have kept their specific names and are not duplicates.

By the time Audubon wrote to Bachman from the Floridas, aboard a revenue cutter on an expedition, they both knew Holbrook very well. "The island [of Barataria, Grande Terre] abounds with snakes—not, however, injurious excepting a very small *ground* Rattle species," he said in 1837. "We have placed several in rum for Doctor Holbrook and Crabs for yourself. No insects of note except *Musquitoes* and sand flies, of which we could spare enough, God knows." A week before, he had mentioned excellent "Alligator hunting on a fine Bayou" near New Orleans, admitting that its flesh, for eating, was "far from being bad." "God preserve us from ever 'riding' a live one . . . after all, they are not to be fooled with," he concluded.

It would appear that at some time in the next few years Audubon's ideas about Holbrook underwent an unfavorable change, if one is to judge by a letter of 1841 to the painter from John Bachman, who was not, himself, exactly complimentary to the professor: ". . . I am sorry you give so bad an account of friend Holbrook, but I will give you a short episode which may possibly induce you to think more favorably of his *professorship.* Some weeks ago he called during my absence and borrowed my gun from Mrs. Bachman. He did not return it for some days. When he brought it back with the stock broke in two, he never said a word about the accident. When I charged him with it, he laughed and said some of the visitors at his farm had broken it. When I asked him who they were he said he could not in honor tell me. So I have eighteen dollars, for my wife's good nature, to pay. I tell the story everywhere to my friends and repeat it to him, and he laughs most heartily. Never mind, I shall mark him yet."

Nevertheless, Bachman and his sister-in-law Maria were of service to Holbrook, as the acknowledgments in his first volume testify. He thanked Bachman for his "interesting remarks," particularly on the habits of the alligator.

Because of the steady recurrence of Holbrook's name in the Bachman letter collection in Charleston, the author considered it advisable to turn to his rare book on reptiles, with an eye to possible mention of Audubon. In it Holbrook was found to speak highly of the garish little snake in the chuck-will's-widow bird plate by the painter. It was startling to come upon six turtles and tortoises "Drawn on Stone by George Lehman," who painted landscape backgrounds for some of Audubon's birds. Even more surprising was the discovery that Maria Martin had provided Holbrook with "some accurate and very spirited drawings of Carolina reptiles," one of which, the "Coluber constrictor," or blacksnake, he published.

Picture the delicate, "white-faced" Miss Martin, who excelled at drawing insects and flowers, calmly seated before the menacing blacksnake which she seems to have drawn from life. It is coiled as if about to spring. The Bachman letter collection reveals how creatures in variety were kept caged alive, or bottled, in the Charleston mansion for study. Harmless to humans, the snake which engaged Maria's attention was nevertheless, as Holbrook remarked, "irascible" if teased. Most of the illustrations were by an Italian-born artist, J. Sera, who was engaged about 1826 and remained with Holbrook until his death in 1832, ten years before the work was finished.

Holbrook would permit only live or fresh specimens as models. He had the illustrations lithographed and added to his gradually produced text in no special scientific order, though he evidently kept, more or less, the arrangement practiced by his old Paris friends, Duméril and Bibron, somewhat in mind as he proceeded. He did the best that he could, but the result, while enjoying the distinction of being the first such senior effort among our pioneers, is now reckoned as superficial and confusing. His deficiencies are more than forgivable when one considers the primitive state of communications, as well as the scarcity of library resources and museum materials, not only in Charleston but throughout the states.

The appearance of Holbrook's work in 1842, before the annexation of Texas and California, worked decidedly in that author's favor, for those territories doubled our reptilian species. He was very frankly conscious of all the handicaps and he freely cited them, admitting in his preface a fear of "describing animals as new" which were long since known to European naturalists. "In no department of American zoology," he averred, "is there so much confusion as in herpetology."

Holbrook abandoned his plans for including an anatomical supplement to his work. But by 1855, his outlook brighter, he began to publish an ambitious project on fishes, one which was to furnish him with even greater difficulties than his first publishing venture.

l'Affaire Rattlesnake

No popular hero has been the victim of more invidious and trivial whispering campaigns than, perhaps, John James Audubon, nevertheless beloved of millions of his countrymen. This truth obtains now as in the past. Scientists have been his special critics.

While accomplishing his first staggering ambition—that of publishing 1,065 distinct bird figures in 435 separate aquatint prints, and writing biographies to go with them—he never stopped searching for new species, drawing and redrawing, correcting engravings, transporting weighty portfolios up and down the Atlantic coast and across the ocean and the English Channel while seeking subscribers to keep his project going. That he *did* perpetrate some errors was not only a very human consequence of such vast aims, but an inevitable one. Even so, some of the few imprecise details of his plates are chargeable to Havell's staff engravers, particularly where they occur in the drawing of "bills, legs and feet," as Audubon's explosive criticism indicated in letters to Havell.

Occasionally in the field Audubon mistook the young of certain birds for new species. And two or three of his bird drawings raise the question of authenticity, the birds never having been seen by others. Be that as it may, some of his most mordant critics, few of whom have contributed one quarter as much to American ornithology, enjoy such modern advantages as trains, cars, speed cameras, sensitive binoculars, recording apparatus, and much else besides to facilitate their research. Apart from the fact that few of them can paint or draw, almost none can turn out prose as fresh as Audubon's, the naturalist's ghost-writing services notwithstanding. MacGillivray himself, when he wrote on birds independently of his editing services to Audubon, was accused of borrowing the best of his American associate's style! As he penciled away the asperities in the painter's biographies of birds, he assured their author that he was as good a writer as he was artist. But new recruits for the old cabal periodically raise their voices in protest, while the chorus of Audubon's vast following engulfs and drowns the voices of his critics. Stanley Clisby Arthur, himself a naturalist of reputation, once wisely observed that "unfriendly feelings and charges and counter charges by ornithologists and naturalists have not altered much in the past hundred and twenty-five years."

This brings us to the sharpest controversy of Audubon's career, one which stemmed both from a paper, "Notes on the Rattlesnake," which he read before the Wernerian Society of Edinburgh, and his picture of mockingbirds attacked in their nest by that creature (Plate XXI in the *Birds*).* The paper was drafted from a large accumulation of notes made for years by the naturalist, such as this diary entry dated October 25, 1821, at Oakley plantation in West Feliciana:

"Finished drawing a very fine Specimen of a Rattle Snake that measured 5 feet 7/12 inches, weighed 6 1/4 lbs. and had 10 Rattles. Anxious to give it

* See page 100.

such a position as I thought would render it most interesting to a naturalist, I put it in that which the reptile generally takes when on the point of inflicting a most severe wound. I have examined the fangs of many before, and their position along the superior jaw bones, but had never seen one showing the whole exposed. . . . On dissection I found them strongly attached as follows. . . . "

Here Audubon gave a minutely detailed description of the fangs and the venom process in relation to the jawbones. It was soon to serve as his answer to those critics who challenged his powers of observation (a purpose which it would also admirably serve today). After listing the measurements, the number of scales, and the like, Audubon added these lines to the entry: "My drawing will, I hope, give you a good idea of a rattlesnake, although the heat of the weather would not permit me to spend more than 16 hours at it. My amiable pupil, Miss Eliza Pirrie, also drew the same snake." He was referring to his young drawing pupil of Oakley plantation. The snake thus described was redrawn for Plate XXI.

Proudly full of his firsthand knowledge, Audubon accepted the invitation of the Wernerian Society to read a paper on the habits of the rattlesnake on February 10, 1828. Then, unprepared at the last moment, he confessed in his journal: "I was sorry that I was not prepared to read to those assembled that a rattle snake rattled his tail, not to give knowledge to man of his presence, but because he never strikes without rattling, and that, destitute of that appendage, he cannot strike at all." He closed the entry with a note of premonitory sadness: "The wind blows a doleful tune and I feel utterly alone." By February 24 he was ready to speak, or so he thought. His paper blew not only a "doleful tune" but a first-rate tempest as things turned out. Added to that was the effect of the snake in Plate XXI, which helped whip up the storm of protest.

"To the Wernerian Society at two o'clock," he wrote in his journal in the evening, "my drawing of the Mocking-bird with me. The room was completely filled and a paper on the rhubarb of commerce was read, then Professor Jameson called my name. I rose, and read as distinctly as I could my paper on Rattle snakes, a job of three quarters of an hour. Having finished I was cheered by all, and the thanks of the Assembly was unanimously voted. My cheeks burned, and after a few questions had been put to me I handed my manuscript to Professor Jameson, and was glad to be gone." He went on to an exhibition of paintings at the "Scottish Society," but soon left there rather than endure the gaze of "so many eyes" upon him.

Charles Waterton, a close English friend of the leader of the Alexander Wilson coterie in Philadelphia, George Ord, led the attack that followed in the British press. London newspapers quoted Waterton's assertion that Audubon's rattlesnake reports, both painted and written, were only so much nonsense by an American inventor of falsehoods, more outrageous than those of the professional prevaricator Baron Münchhausen. Waterton said the gaping jaws of the snake attacking birds in the picture could be those of only a "fabulous hydra." To him, as to others then and now, the nest of the mockingbirds seemed to be in a tree, though actually the flowering shrub in the painting is a jessamine bush with the nest in it just above the ground, in the path of the rattler.

In the paper that he read, Audubon had told of seeing a rattlesnake pursue a squirrel up and down a tree and kill it by rolling itself about the little animal. Waterton scoffed at this story.

Ord, the Philadelphia press, and scientific journals took up the cry, Ord ridiculing the "recurved" fangs of the snake in the painting, pronouncing them a fabrication upon the truer shape of fangs with downward curving tips which he had examined in South America in similar reptiles. He too said the rattler was not a climber.

In the ensuing years, as the argument blew hot and cold, an outraged Audubon sought the testimony of his friends about the climbing rattlesnake. Thomas Sully, an American painter as famous then as now, being in London in 1827, wrote to Audubon who was in Edinburgh to report what his mail from Philadelphia had been containing of interest about the rattlesnake scandal. In injured tones the naturalist replied that his professional ethics had been impugned—and impugned unjustly:

". . . I am not much astonished that in Philadelphia remarks should have been made respecting some papers read by me to different institutions in this country, but I am grieved at it. . . . The greatest portion of my life has been devotedly spent in the active investigation of nature. . . . This arduous task I have followed with unremitting diligence, and with industry that has caused my family and myself more troubles than any person in Philadelphia can be aware of. For more than twenty years I have been in *the regular habit* of writing down every day all the incidents of which I have been an *eye-witness,* on the spot, and without confiding to my memory. You have read some portion of this journal, and have also been an eye-witness to many of the occurrences, but my dear Mr. Sully you are not the only evidence. Mr. Joseph Mason . . . accompanied me on a hunting excursion in Louisiana which lasted eighteen months. Captain Cummings, author of a treatise on the navigation of the Ohio and Mississippi, was one of the party, and he saw me write in my journal. My family has seen the whole of these diaries, and could readily assert the truth of their contents, to much of which they were a party, present and acting. The papers are merely copies from those journals . . . transcribed . . . and corrected.

"Those persons in Philadelphia that have felt a desire to contradict my assertions cannot . . . conceive that the Wernerian Society would have listened to my 'say so' without my having investigated the subject. Neither can the Society believe that all my particular friends would permit me to relate *Tales of Wonder* which, if untrue, would load me with disgrace, ruin of family, nay prove me devoid of all honor! Could I suffer myself to be blinded at the very moment when I am engaged in the publication of a work of unparalleled magnitude . . . ? No, my dear Mr. Sully, I have written with care what I have seen, and have felt a great desire to spread the knowledge I have obtained. . . . I have not read any of the Philadelphia papers since I came to England, but judging from your friendly letter, I feel assured that the pen that traced them must have been dipped in venom more noxious than that which flows from the jaws of the rattlesnake! . . ."

Another artist strengthened Audubon's confidence in his own ability, and, quite by chance, the controversial mockingbird plate was singled out by him for praise. The artist François Gérard, best French portraitist of his day, saw the *Birds* when the naturalist took them to Paris. Introduced by Redouté, as Audubon's journal relates, Gérard greeted him with, "Welcome, Brother in Arts." "All curiosity to see my drawings," Audubon related, "he took up the one of the Mocking-birds, and offering me his hand, said: 'Mr. Audubon, you are the king of ornithological painters. We are all children in France and in Europe. Who would have expected such things from the woods of America?'" Gérard's interest in Audubon was undoubtedly heightened by the fact that both of them at different times in their youth had been pupils of Jacques Louis David.

Back again in the States for a visit in 1831, Audubon wrote to Lucy from St. Augustine, Florida, with as much feeling as ever on the sensitive subject: "The scribblers about Rattle snake *stories* will now have to hang their ears and shut their invidious mouths. Hast thou read the letter of Colonel J. J. Abert to Harlan and published in *Franklin Journal?* I have a more extraordinary account in store respecting these reptiles. One was found in this place, twisted around the top of a mahogany bed post in the chamber of a most venerable lady, and I have a certificate well attested to of that fact." Abert later told Audubon that he had not only seen rattlers "climbing trees but being shot on them." The word of this well-known explorer and member of the roving U.S. Topographical Engineers had no little weight.

Old Thomas Cooper, president of South Carolina College, whose rotund form, frock coat, and broad-brimmed hat are known to all admirers of the celebrated silhouettes by Brown, bore witness in his favor. The South Carolinian told him that he had seen a rattler climb a five-rail fence on his land. By 1837 Audubon was writing jubilantly to young Spencer Fullerton Baird, destined for fame with the Smithsonian, that Colonel James Morgan, another explorer of note, had given him a specimen with *"double* recurved fangs," which would not only confirm his own reports but also "prove a new genus." That dealt the *coup de grâce* to Ord's argument.

As for Waterton's ceaseless attacks on the painter's veracity—and they numbered nineteen altogether—anything might be expected of such an eccentric. The lord of Walton Hall lived on a pittance equal to that of a laborer on his land, slept on the floor with an oaken block for a pillow, retired at eight, rose at three to pray, and was dressed at dawn and roaming his 260 acres, studying birds and mammals. He had spent fifty thousand dollars on a wall to fence in the creatures and shut himself away from prying eyes of humans. He spent his spare time preparing diatribes against other naturalists, managing in spite of all his polemics to do serious scientific good in his choleric eighty-three years.

The rattler's ghost was not yet laid, however. In 1910, in a communication to the *Scientific American* answering one of Audubon's later critics, one George W. Colles raised the possibility that the reptile in the story of the squirrel chase was a blacksnake. Mr. Colles wrote:

"With one exception the naturalist's remarks are absolutely in accord with the known habits of our common snakes, the exception being that Audubon mistook his species. The snake which pursued and caught the squirrel was evidently not a rattlesnake but a common blacksnake, the 'blue-racer.' This, to be sure, is a rather gross error, and shows Audubon was more familiar with birds, but from a mistake to a lie is a far cry. The fact that he mistook a blacksnake for a rattlesnake does not prove anything versus the truth of his story. In fact, it is inconceivable that a scientist of such a thoroughly grounded reputation for accuracy in detail could be guilty of manufacturing such a story, even if it were possible that he could invent one so absolutely in accordance with facts, without knowing the facts. Read blacksnake for rattlesnake, and the story is absolutely accurate. I have observed every one of the elements of the narration personally. . . . How could a snake 'rattle' having no rattles? The blacksnake vibrates the end of its tail, and in dry leaves, against a log, etc., this produces a rattling sound. Darwin alludes to this habit—of the copperhead—to explain the evolution of rattles.

"It is certainly strange that Audubon should not have observed *with surprise* that the snake killed his prey by constriction instead of by poison. But it must be supposed that the rattling was what deluded him and convinced him that he was dealing with a rattlesnake."

At the turn of the century the blacksnake in question was commonly known as the blue racer, as in Colles' reply, which was received with respect and which still holds water but for his use of the word "constriction." Until recent times that word has been drawn upon to describe the method of the blacksnake's predatory operations, which involve coiling about its prey but not killing by constricting. Colles used the word "constriction." Audubon did not. But for the word "rattlesnake," instead of "blacksnake," Audubon's account, in the view of Mr. Colles, passes muster.

This account of the naturalist's misadventures with rattlesnakes can end on a wryly humorous note, thanks to John Bachman. When the Lutheran minister and scientist had finally had quite enough of the long-drawn-out argument, he sat down and wrote a communication to the editor of the *Bucks County Intelligencer,* which had figured in the upheaval.

"Audubon has been rudely assailed about a 'snake story' but Waterton has given us several stories that fairly fill us with wonder and dismay. Instead of a contemptible rattlesnake, as thick as a man's arm, he tells us of a great 'Boa' which he encountered in his den. Dashing headlong on the Boa, he pierced him with his lance and tying up his mouth carried him as a trophy to the British Museum. The snake was so large that it took three men to carry it, and so heavy that they had to rest three times.

"He gives another snake story—a snake ten feet long. Waterton was alone. He seized him by the tail, the snake turned around and came after him with open mouth, seeming to say, 'What business have you to meddle with my tail!' In this emergency, he put his fist in his hat and rammed it down the snake's throat. Suffering the snake to wind itself around his body, he walked home in triumph. . . . I am somewhat indifferent with regard to Mr. Waterton and his marvelous book. But it is well for the public to know who this champion of truth is, that comes to accuse the American Ornithologist of exaggeration."

All ears and eyes focused on the controversial aspects of Audubon and the rattlesnake, with the result that the remainder of the address he delivered on that fateful February 24, 1827, has long since been forgotten. Vivid and colorful, it includes his report on the torpidity of snakes, never revived since its appearance in the *Edinburgh New Philosophical Journal,* which published "Notes on the Rattlesnake" that year.[1]

"Periodical torpidity in snakes," wrote Audubon, "has been wisely ordered, on acount of the very slow growth granted to most of them. Snakes, as well as alligators, increase in size very slowly, and are consequently long-lived. . . .

"Augustin Bourgeat, my younger son John Woodhouse and myself were hunting one winter day for ducks. Near a lake we struck up a fire and began picking and cleaning our game for what we were pleased to call our dinner. My son, running about for wood, discovered a rattlesnake so large, closely coiled up by a log in a torpid state that he called us to come and look at it . . . stiff as a stone.

"At my request my son put it into my game bag on my back. Whilst our game was roasting on the wooden forks stuck in front of our cheerful fire, I felt something moving behind me. The time taken in unstrapping and throwing off the bag with the reptile in it was, I assure you, of short duration. The snake, quite alive, issued from the bag and began rattling with its head elevated, its body closely coiled to defend itself from all attacks. A distance from the fire it stopped its alarum and was bent on finding a place of refuge, again to become torpid. After we finished our meal, my son, who had been watching all the snake's movements with the eagerness of youth, brought it back again with a smile, saying, 'Papa, look at Hercules and the serpent!'

"We took it home, and it became torpid or revived at our pleasure as often as we moved or brought it near the fire, until, in a jar of spirits where we put it, it travelled to the Lyceum of New York. . . .

"One of the most wonderful faculties possessed by this and many other species of snake is that of being able to live without any food whatever for years. Quite as remarkable it is that their appearance scarcely exhibits any signs of want. Yet their movements, power of rattling and of inflicting mortal wounds are perfectly kept up. One which I confined in a cage for three years had rats, young rabbits and birds put in with it—sometimes alive —without their ever being touched. The snake made no move to approach.

"The operation of throwing off its skin annually was abandoned by this snake after the first spring of confinement. . . . During the whole time, it did not grow in the least. I have thought that this power of abstinence

[1] It also published his paper on the alligator in 1826-1827.

might go far towards proving that it had not that of fascination. It would be very unnatural for an animal so gifted to lie and suffer while the single glance of a magnetic eye could bring down a bird at once from the top of any tree into its mouth.

"I now and then turned the snake out of its cage. With great quickness it would go about the room, looking in all directions, with a view to effecting its escape. As I was armed with a stick, it never made towards me, but if I put myself in its way it would stop, prepare for action, and rattle, until I moved and afforded it a free passage.

"Rattlesnakes are easily disabled. A single smart blow, even of a slender twig, will disjoint any part of the vertebrae, after which they lie at your mercy. . . .

"Can we for a moment imagine that the Creator has exposed the feathered race to such dangers as the power of fascination would imply? We may rest assured that snakes destroy birds and animals by the quickness of their motion and the acuteness of their sight, seconded by cunning and strength, but never by fascination."

Nearly twenty years later when he was writing about the Carolina gray squirrel for the *Quadrupeds,* Audubon, still firmly convinced of his own veracity, repeated what he had said in his earlier address about a rattlesnake's pursuit of a squirrel into a tree, and about its victory not by venom but constriction. Climbing and constriction are blacksnake feats, but Audubon would not back down. He added an absorbing essay on the alleged powers of these two creatures, almost entirely forgetting the little squirrel:

"Some persons have attributed a mysterious power—more especially to the rattlesnake and blacksnake—*fascinating,* or *charming.* . . . The basilisk of the ancients killed by a look. The eye of the rattlesnake is supposed to paralyze and at the same time attract its intended prey. The animal slowly approaches, advancing and retreating until it finally falls powerless into the open jaws of its devourer.

"As long as we are able to explain, by natural deductions, the very singular maneuvers of birds and squirrels when 'fascinated' by a snake, it would be absurd to imagine that anything mysterious or supernatural is connected with the subject. . . . Fear and surprise cause an instinctive horror when we find ourselves unexpectedly within a foot or two of a rattlesnake. The shrill, startling noise from the rattles of its tail as it vibrates rapidly, and its hideous aspect, no doubt produce a much greater effect on birds and small quadrupeds. It is said that the distant roar of the African lion causes the oxen to tremble and stand paralyzed in the fields. Humboldt relates that in the forests of South America the mingled cries of monkeys and other animals resound through the whole night. But as soon as the roar of the jaguar is heard, terror seizes on all the other animals, and their voices are suddenly hushed. Birds and quadrupeds are very curious, also, and their feeling prompts them to draw near to strange objects. . . .

"The Indians attract the reindeer [caribou], the antelope and other animals until they are within bow-shot, by waving a stick with a red cloth attached to it, or by throwing themselves on their backs and kicking their heels up in the air.

"If any strange object is thrown into the poultry yard all the fowls will crowd near it and scrutinize it for a long time. Everybody, almost, may have observed at some time or other dozens of birds collected around a cat in shrubbery, a tortoise, or, particularly, a snake.

"The Squirrel is remarkable for its fondness for 'sights,' and will sometimes come down from the highest branch of a tree to within three feet of the ground to take a look at a small scarlet snake not much larger than a pipe-stem, and which, having no poisonous fangs, could scarcely master a grasshopper. This might be regarded as a decided case in favor of theories on the fascinating powers of snakes. But the following circumstances which happened to me would be difficult to explain in that way.

"After observing a squirrel come down to inspect just such a little scarlet snake, the reptile, being a rare species, I captured and put in the carriage box. After driving off I recollected that I had left my box of botanical specimens at the place where I had first seen the snake. On returning I saw the squirrel darting backward and forward, skipping round the root of the tree, eyeing with equal curiosity the article I had left behind. I could not help reflecting that if the little snake had 'charmed' the squirrel, the same 'fascinating' influence was exercised by my tin box!

"Quadrupeds and birds have certain antipathies. They are capable of experiencing many of the feelings of mankind—susceptible of passion—sometimes spiteful and revengeful—wise to their 'natural enemies' without a formal introduction. The blue jay, brown thrush, white-eyed flycatcher and other little birds are often to be heard scolding, and fluttering about a thicket in which some animal is concealed. If you examine the cause of their excitement you will probably see a wild cat or fox spring forth from the covert. Everyone must have seen the owl or buzzard chased by the smallest birds, which united to drive off a common enemy. The birds sometimes approach too near, and are seized by the owl. I once watched some night-hawks darting round a tree in which an owl was perched. The owl made a sudden movement, caught a hawk in his sharp claws, and notwithstanding the cries and menaces of the others he instantly devoured it.

"Birds dart in the same manner at snakes, and no doubt are often caught by passing too near. Shall we, therefore, conclude that they are fascinated?

"One of the most powerful 'attractions' which remain to be considered is the love of offspring. This feeling, so deeply rooted in the system of nature as to be a rule, almost without exception, is manifested strongly by birds and quadrupeds. Snakes are among the most dreaded destroyers of eggs and young birds, and of the young of small animals. Is it not likely, therefore, that many of the supposed cases of fascination may be referred to the intrepidity of the animals or birds, trying to defend their young or to drive away their enemy from their vicinity?

"In the *Birds of America* I represented a mocking-bird's nest attacked by a rattlesnake, and the nest of a red thrush invaded by a black-snake. The two plates show several birds assisting the pair of birds whose nest has been robbed by the snake, and also show the mocking-bird and thrush courageously advancing even to the jaws of their enemy. These pictures were drawn after the actual occurrence before my eyes. A person but little acquainted with natural history might readily fancy that at least some of these birds were fascinated. . . ."

Now for the account of the less flaccid rattler which Audubon kept in captivity—the creature which did not disdain to touch what was put before it.

"I have more to say of the habits of the rattlesnake in this connection. I have seen one, kept in a very large cage, use every means within its power and exert its cunning for a whole month before it succeeded in capturing a brown thrush imprisoned with it. At night the bird roosted beyond the reach of the snake. By day it was too cautious and too agile—snatching up its food at intervals and flying instantly back to its perch—to be struck by the unwieldy serpent. This experiment offered a fair opportunity for the rattlesnake to exert its powers of fascination, had it possessed any. But as it did not exhibit them, we do not hesitate to say that it was entirely destitute of any faculty of the kind. . . ."

Finally, the rattler took up its station beside the water cup. What occurred on the third day of its watch is left to the imagination. Audubon now summed up his argument.

"If, notwithstanding these facts, it is argued that the mysterious and inexplicable power of *fascination* is possessed by the snake because birds have been seen to approach it with open wings and plaintive voice, seeming to wait upon its appetite, we must be prepared to admit that the same faculty is possessed by other animals. I once saw a mocking-bird, behaving as birds are said to do under the influence of fascination, approach a hog which was munching something at the foot of a small cedar. The bird fluttered before the grunter with open wings, uttered a low and plaintive note, alighted on his back and began to peck at his snout—only because she had a nest in the tree from which several of her younglings had fallen. A friend informed me of a similar scene between a cat-bird and a dog which had disturbed her brood. The bird went through many of those movements generally ascribed to the effect of fascination."

Bird and Reptile in West Feliciana

In his biography of the reptile-hunting wood ibis, Audubon gives us a vivid picture of the Bayou Sarah region of Louisiana, or the setting of Oakley plantation which, with Beech Woods, is the provenance of the sketchbook. The small reptiles among the sketches undoubtedly came from the very haunts of this bird, whose history, as told in *Ornithological Biography,* is a masterpiece of nature writing.

"The country which the wood ibis inhabits is suited to its habits . . . vast and numerous swamps, lagoons, bayous and savannahs that occur in the lower parts of our southern states, all abounding with fishes and reptiles. . . .

"I have seen flocks of several thousands. There is a natural necessity for their flocking together. This species feeds entirely on fish and aquatic reptiles, of which it destroys more than it eats, leaving the balance for alligators, crows and vultures. To procure its food it walks through shallow muddy lakes or bayous in numbers. As soon as the ibises discover a place abounding in fish, they dance all through it, until the water becomes thick with mud stirred by their feet. In the course of ten or fifteen minutes, hundreds of fishes, frogs, young alligators and water snakes cover the surface. The birds greedily swallow them, then walk to the nearest margins, place themselves in long rows with their breasts all turned towards the sun in the manner of pelicans and vultures, and remain thus for an hour or so. Then they all take wing, rise in spirals to an immense height, and sail about for perhaps an hour, performing the most beautiful evolutions that can well be imagined. Their long legs and necks are stretched out, and their white plumage contrasts beautifully with the jet black tips of their wings. Now in large circles they ascend to the upper regions; now they pitch toward the earth; again they gently rise, renewing their gyrations. Hunger once more induces them to go in search of food, and they sail rapidly towards another lake or bayou, through canebrake, cypress swamp, and tangled wood.

"Follow their course, reader. Seldom do they return to the same feeding place on the same day. Picture yourself standing on the margin of a dark-watered bayou, leading off in a labyrinth of complete darkness. The tall canes bow from the shores. The majestic trees above, all hung with funereal lichen, gently wave in the suffocating atmosphere. The bullfrog, alarmed, sinks into the water. The alligator raises his head above the surface, probably to see if the ibises have arrived, and the wily cougar stealthily advances towards one of the birds, expecting to carry it off into the thicket. In the dim light you discern the white plumage moving rapidly about like specters. The loud clacking of the mandibles or jaws of the ibises apprises you of the havoc they are committing among the terrified inhabitants of the waters. Move at all and you invariably lose your opportunity to observe their actions. Some old male has detected you, whether with eye or ear does not matter. The first stick your foot cracks, his hoarse voice sounds the alarm. Off they go, battering down the bending cane with their powerful pinions, and breaking tree twigs as they force their way out.

"Talk to me of the stupidity of birds, of the dullness of the wood ibis! Say it is fearless, easily approached, and easily shot. I listen, but merely through courtesy. I have so repeatedly watched its movements in all kinds of circumstances that I am quite convinced we have not in the United States a more shy, wary and vigilant bird.

"In the two years which, I may say, I spent among them while living near Bayou Sarah, I never succeeded in surprising one, even under cover of night, when they were roosting on trees nearly a hundred feet high, sometimes in swamps. . . .

"One of the most curious circumstances connected with this ibis is that although the birds, when feeding, are almost constantly within the reach of large alligators, whose young they devour, these reptiles never attack them. But if a duck or heron comes within reach of their tails it is immediately killed and swallowed. The wood ibis will wade up to its belly in water, round the edge of 'alligators' holes,' without ever being injured. Should one of these birds be shot, however, an alligator immediately makes towards it and pulls it under water. The gar-fish is not so courteous, but gives chase to the ibises whenever an opportunity occurs. The snapping-turtle is also a great enemy to the young of the ibis. . . .

"Besides the great quantity of fishes that these birds destroy, they also devour frogs, young alligators, wood rats, young rails and grackles, fiddlers and other crabs as well as snakes and small turtles. They never eat the eggs of the alligator as has been alleged, although they probably could do so if they were able to demolish the matted nests of that animal, a task beyond *any* bird known to me. When they are eating, the clacking of their jaws can be heard at a distance of several hundred yards. . . . The wood ibis takes four years to attain full maturity, although birds are now and then found breeding in their second year. This is rare, however, because the young live in flocks by themselves until they attain about the age of three years. In the fourth year it appears as you see it in the *Birds of America*."

BIBLIOGRAPHY

Books and Periodicals

Abert, Colonel John J. "Habits of Climbing of the Rattlesnake." A letter to Dr. Richard Harlan of Philadelphia, published in part in *Monthly American Journal of Geology and Natural Science,* vol. 1, pp. 221-223, 1832.

Arthur, Stanley Clisby, *Audubon, an Intimate Life of the American Woodsman.* New Orleans, 1937.

Audubon, John James. *The Birds of America.* Text. Royal octavo. 7 vols. New York and Philadelphia, 1840-1844.

Audubon, John James. *Ornithological Biography.* 5 vols. Edinburgh, 1831-1839.

Audubon, John James. *Letters of John James Audubon, 1826-1840.* 2 vols. Howard Corning, ed. Boston, The Club of Odd Volumes, 1930.

Audubon, John James. "Notes on the Rattlesnake." In *Edinburgh New Philosophical Journal,* vol. 3, pp. 21-30, April-Oct., 1827.

Audubon, John James. "Observations on the Natural History of the Alligator." In a letter to Sir William Jardine, published in the *Edinburgh New Philosophical Journal,* vol. 2, pp. 270-280, Oct.-April, 1826-1827.

Audubon, John James, and Bachman, the Rev. John. *The Viviparous Quadrupeds of North America.* "Carolina Gray Squirrel"; passage on "powers of fascination," vol. 1, pp. 58-62, 1846.

Audubon, John James. *Journal of John James Audubon, 1820-1821.* Howard Corning, ed. Boston, The Club of Odd Volumes, 1929.

Audubon, Lucy, ed. *The Life and Adventures of John James Audubon, the Naturalist.* Introduction by James Grant Wilson. New York, 1869. A slightly revised version of Buchanan's biography below.

Audubon, Maria R., and Coues, Elliott. *Audubon and His Journals.* 2 vols. New York, 1897.

Buchanan, Robert. *The Life and Adventures of John James Audubon, the Naturalist.* London, 1868. Edited with materials supplied by Lucy Audubon, wife of the naturalist.

Breck, Samuel. *Recollections . . . (1771-1862).* London, 1870.

Call, R. E. *The Life and Writings of Constantine Rafinesque.* Filson Club Publications, no. 10, pp. 24-29. Louisville, 1895.

Colles, George W. "A Defense of Audubon." *Scientific American,* vol. 98, p. 311, 1908.

Gill, Theodore. "Biographical Memoir of John Edwards Holbrook, 1794-1871." Read before the National Academy of Sciences and published in its *Biographical Memoirs,* vol. 5, pp. 47-77, 1905.

Hagen, H. A. "The First Numero of Thomas Say's American Entomology . . ." *Psyche,* pp. 145-146, March, 1884.

Herrick, Francis Hobart. *Audubon the Naturalist, a History of His Life and Time.* 2 vols. New York, 1917. Reissued in one volume in 1938, with an introduction on Audubon and the "Lost Dauphin" controversy.

Holbrook, John Edwards. *Herpetology of the United States.* 5 vols. Charleston, 1835-1837, 1842 (complete).

Hutt, W. N. "Audubon the Original Nature Fakir." *Scientific American,* vol. 98, p. 59. 1908.

James, Edwin. *Account of an Expedition from Pittsburgh to the Rocky Mountains.* Philadelphia and London, 1823.

Jones, Thomas P. "The Romance of the Rattlesnake." *Franklin Journal & American Mechanics Magazine,* vol. 2. n.s., p. 144, Aug., 1828.

Jordan, David Starr. "Rafinesque." *Popular Science Monthly,* vol. 29, no. 11, pp. 212-221, June, 1886.

Jordan, David Starr. "A Review of Rafinesque's Memoirs. . . ." *Contributions to North American Ichthyology,* I, pp. 6. U. S. National Museum, Washington, D. C., 1877.

Le Conte, John L., ed. *The Complete Writings of Thomas Say on the Entomology of North America.* With a memoir of Say by George Ord. 2 vols. London, 1859.

Melsheimer, F. V. *A Catalogue of Insects of Pennsylvania.* York, Pa., 1806. Earliest American publication on North American insects.

Neal, John. [An attack on Audubon for his alleged unfairness to Joseph Mason.] In *New England Galaxy,* vol. 18, no. 16, April 18, 1835.

Nölte, Vincent. *Fifty Years in Both Hemispheres: or Reminiscences of a Merchant's Life.* London, 1854.

Peattie, Donald Culross. *Audubon's America.* New York, 1940. Contains long excerpts from Audubon's journals of 1820-1821.

Richards, I. T. "Audubon, Joseph R. Mason, and John Neal." *American Literature,* vol. 6, pp. 122-140, 1934.

Rosengarten, J. G. *French Colonists and Exiles in the United States.* Philadelphia, 1907. Includes Charles A. Lesueur, Audubon's friend.

Say, Thomas. *American Entomology.* 3 vols. Philadelphia, 1824-1828. First American book publication on North American insects.

Teale, Edwin Way. "Audubon's Insects." *Audubon Magazine,* vol. 49, no. 6, pp. 323-331, Nov.-Dec., 1947.

Waterton, Charles. "A Letter to James Jameson, Esq." Privately printed in Wakefield, England, 1835. An attack both on Audubon and Jameson's Defense of his snake stories. Reprinted in *Essays on Natural History;* London, 1871.

Youmans, William J. *Pioneers of Science in America.* New York, 1896.

Manuscripts and Letters

Arthur, Stanley Clisby. Private correspondence with Bertha Bowen concerning Audubon's sketchbook. Notebook with transcript of annotations on original drawings for *The Birds of America.*

American Philosophical Society, Philadelphia, Pa. Letters of Audubon, his family and associates. Ms. of the episode, "The Fair Incognito." Unpublished pages of the 1820-1821 journal.

Chambers, Mrs. Kirby. Transcript of portions of the memoirs of Mrs. Charles Basham, original owner of the sketchbook presented by Audubon.

The Charleston Museum, Charleston, S. C. Bachman letter collection. Sketchbook copies of Say's *American Entomology,* plus other water colors from nature by Maria Martin.

Houghton Library of Harvard University, Cambridge, Mass. Audubon letters; letters of his family and associates. Early water-color sketches of birds by Audubon, including insect details.

The Smithsonian Institution, Washington, D. C. Photographic copies of Rafinesque's notebook with copies of Audubon's "impossible fishes."

INDEX

Entries printed in SMALL CAPITALS refer to illustrations.

Entries printed in SMALL CAPITALS refer to illustrations.

Entries printed in SMALL CAPITALS refer to illustrations.

Entries printed in SMALL CAPITALS refer to illustrations.